Pra

LOVE SLOWS DOWN

"It's easy to confuse a lot of activity with a purposeful life. Sometimes we get so busy doing good things that we don't have room for the best thing—loving others with focused intention. In *Love Slows Down*, my friend Joël leads us on a great adventure—the journey of learning how to overcome fear and anger and hurt so you're free to slow down and truly live love."

BOB GOFF
Founder of Love Does
Honorable Consul of Uganda
Author of *New York Times* bestsellers *Love Does* and *Everybody Always*

"I've been on some amazing adventures with Joël—hiking to Machu Picchu, rafting the Grand Canyon—and I've seen his passion for helping people live in the freedom of their identity in Christ. This book is about the greatest adventure of all: walking in God's love that sets us free from fear and anger. It's filled with personal stories of adventure and triumph that will challenge and inspire you to live with courage and confidence."

MARK BATTERSON
Pastor of National Community Church in Washington, DC
New York Times bestselling author

"Anger is often a result of disappointment. When things don't turn out the way we expect them to, it's easy to become angry and succumb to fear. In *Love Slows Down*, my friend Joël Malm reminds us all that God's love calms our fears and frees our heart to trust Him—especially when life doesn't make sense."

JOHN BEVERE
Bestselling author and minister
Messenger International

"Every day at the Dream Center I see the miraculous power of what God's love can do. Love can drive out cycles of addiction and anxiety and anger. In *Love Slows Down*, my friend Joël shares lots of life-changing stories and principles that can help you unleash the power of God's love in all your most important relationships."

MATTHEW BARNETT
Pastor and co-founder of the Dream Center

"Joël Malm is one of the most adventurous and authentic people on the planet. In his powerful new book, *Love Slows Down*, he invites readers on a Kilimanjaro-sized adventure of living life to the fullest by letting go of anger and baggage and grabbing hold of faith. We believe this book could instantly and positively impact your faith, your family, your career, and every other part of your life."

DAVE AND ASHLEY WILLIS
Hosts of *The Naked Marriage Podcast*
Bestselling authors of *The Naked Marriage*

"Anger is like a bright flare shooting into the night. It's meant to make us stop and take notice. Too often, we blaze by flashes of anger. Yet ignoring anger never makes it go away. Joël Malm challenges us to take a close look at the source of our anger—the underlying disappointments and hurts—that we may find the healing and wholeness our souls crave. If you've ever wrestled with anger, this book is for you."

MARGARET FEINBERG
Host of *The Joycast*
Author of *Taste and See*

"Joël not only leads adventure trips around the world, he's an expert guide for the interior life. In this age of rush and hurry, *Love Slows Down* is a needed invitation to stop and examine your life. What makes you tick? What makes you ticked off? Your life is a journey. This book will help you travel lighter, carrying what's most important to you and ditching everything else."

ARLENE PELLICANE
Speaker and author of *Parents Rising*

"When we began our ministry of books and speaking on the topic of anger, one of our goals was to destigmatize the issue. Joël Malm does this beautifully in *Love Slows Down*. We're convinced that reading this important book will bring freedom from guilt and the permission to work through your anger issues by loving others—but first by receiving the love of God for *you*, despite your anger. Joël's writing feels like a conversation with a trusted friend who knows your skeletons and is committed to both helping you and encouraging you. A must-read!"

AMBER AND GUY LIA
Coauthors of *Marriage Triggers*
Amber is coauthor of parenting bestsellers *Triggers* and *Parenting Scripts*

Love Slows Down

LOVE
SLOWS
DOWN

How to Keep Anger & Anxiety from Ruining Life's Relationships

JOËL MALM

SALEM
BOOKS
an imprint of Regnery Publishing

Unless otherwise marked, all Scripture references are taken from THE HOLY BIBLE, ENGLISH STANDARD VERSION®. Copyright © 2001 by Crossway, a publishing ministry of Good News Publishers. Used by permission.

Scriptures marked NIV are taken from THE HOLY BIBLE, NEW INTERNATIONAL VERSION®. Copyright © 1973, 1978, 1984, 2011 by Biblica, Inc.™ Used by permission of Zondervan.

Salem Books™ is a trademark of Salem Communications Holding Corporation

Regnery® is a registered trademark of Salem Communications Holding Corporation

ISBN: 978-1-68451-089-4
eISBN: 978-1-68451-101-3

Library of Congress Control Number: 2020932933

Published in the United States by
Salem Books
An Imprint of Regnery Publishing
A Division of Salem Media Group
300 New Jersey Ave NW
Washington, DC 20001
www.SalemBooks.com

Manufactured in the United States of America

10 9 8 7 6 5 4 3 2

Books are available in quantity for promotional or premium use. For information on discounts and terms, please visit our website: www.Regnery.com.

To Elise.

You've slowed me down.

But I love it!

I love you.

CONTENTS

PART I

Consult Your Anger

Love Slows Down. Anger Speeds Up.

Love is patient ...
it is not easily angered.

—*1 Corinthians 13*

L ove is patient.

Most of the time, I am not.

Patient, that is.

Why should I be? We live in a world that pretty much gives me anything I want when I want it. Food. Entertainment. Information. Knowledge.

But there are some things in life that just don't come quickly. In fact, oftentimes those things seem elusive and nearly impossible to get. I'm talking about the big things like love, joy, peace, contentment, fulfillment, and meaning. You want those things for yourself and your family. Love gives, and you're doing your best to give your kids everything you had (or didn't have) growing up. But at times, it seems like the whole world is conspiring to block every goal you have.

We have moments when it seems like things are on track. The relationship seems to be improving. The kids are starting to behave. Things at work have calmed down. You paid all the bills on time this month and had a little left over for fun.

But then it happens.

Whatever *it* is. The disagreement with your spouse. The car accident. A relapse of the illness. The phone call from your child's school. The new project at work. The email from your ex. It throws things back into chaos, and you feel anxious, frustrated, and, well, angry.

Sometimes it just explodes out of nowhere, and your response scares you.

Your kids trigger your anger so quickly that you wonder if there is something really, deeply dangerous lurking inside you.

The raging lunatic you turn into in traffic leaves you feeling guilty and exhausted.

Trying to talk to an actual human on the customer service line brings out the R-rated language you hope your kids never hear you say.

Off-handed comments on social media resonate in your head, and you spend hours thinking about how you can lash out with your own mean responses.

You internalize all your anger about your job, end up feeling worn out all the time, and dread being at work.

Yes, call it frustration or irritation. It's OK to admit it—you feel angry at times.

What's worse, you know anger and anxiety are messing things up in your life.

You notice your kids haven't been quite as willing to talk to you about their struggles since you lost it the last time they confessed. You and your spouse tiptoe around each other at home.

And then there's the anxiety. It's keeping you awake at night. It ruins what should be really enjoyable moments because you're always worried about what could go wrong. You know it's stressing you—and those around you—out.

Anger and anxiety are serious problems, and you know it. (By the way, anger and anxiety are directly connected. More on that shortly.)

It's OK to acknowledge that you're frustrated and anxious. It's OK to admit that your pace of life has become a problem. After all, that's why you picked up this book, right? People who don't realize there's a problem don't read books that mention *slow* or *anger* in the title or subtitle. They just charge ahead, ignore the problem, see it get worse, and then have a meltdown.

And you know you don't want that.

Which is probably what drew you to this book. You see the writing on the wall. You know life is going way too fast. You know you need to slow down. You know you feel angry—a lot. The tension is building. And you know you need to do something about it.

Trust me, you aren't getting any judgment from this side of the page. I've struggled with anxiety and anger most of my life. It's caused lots of regrets and broken relationships. Part of the reason I went to get a master's degree in counseling was to help me sort through my own anger issues. In the process of learning how to help others, I realized that having people sit on a couch and share their fears and hurts with me wasn't my style. So I started leading outdoor adventures instead. A kind of outdoor therapy—hiking to Machu Picchu, climbing Mount Kilimanjaro, rafting the Grand Canyon. My friend Mark Batterson describes what happens on those adventures this way:

Change of Pace + Change of Place = Change of Perspective

When we slow down our busy pace and take some time away, we get a chance to process our lives differently. It brings some clarity and insight.

That's my goal with this book. I don't want to add more to your plate. You're already doing too much! I want to help shift your perspective. I want to help you slow down and see that there's an amazing life full of love, joy, and peace out there, and you don't have time to operate at half-capacity because you're angry and worried. There's too much adventure in life for you to miss out on because you are afraid and offended. You've got people who look up to you. You've got something to give to this world, and worry, frustration, and anger are holding you back.

But they don't have to.

Let me offer some good news. It's possible to live without constant fear and worry. It's possible to control your anger and actually use it for good. Anger is just a sign that something needs to be resolved inside us. Anger isn't bad or sinful. Whenever you feel anger, frustration, or anxiety about what is happening around you, it's always because of something happening inside you. So to deal with anger, you have to learn to look just below the surface at what's going on inside.

Anger is a symptom of fear. Anger and fear (anxiety) are always connected—which is why anger speeds up. When we feel something is threatening us, we kick into a fight-or-flight response that causes our bodies and minds to react and do whatever it takes to confront—or run from—the fear.

But love drives out fear. Which means love is also the solution to your anger. I'll start explaining how shortly.

The question you probably want answered right from the start is this:

Why am I so anxious and angry?

Great question!

Here's the simple answer: it's because you have some hopes and dreams for you and your family, but there are threats all around you to those hopes and dreams. Every hope or dream you have can be narrowed down to one or more of three things:

Security. You want you and your family to be physically and emotionally safe and provided for.

Connection. You want loving relationships, validation, and acceptance from those around you.

Control. You want to feel empowered; you want choices and freedom for you and your family.

We all want the same things.

But everywhere you turn there's something or someone standing in the way of getting those big three. Which is why you're keeping a break-neck pace, doing your best to make sure you and your family achieve those hopes and dreams. When people, situations, or challenges threaten you, they trigger a deep part of you that leads to angry responses.

Fortunately, anger and fear don't have to ruin your life. In fact, anger and fear can become your allies if you learn to use them correctly. They can shine a light on what's holding you back from the life you really want.

Read on and I'll explain...

2

Understand Yourself

*A humble knowledge of thyself is a surer way to God
than a deep search after learning.*

—*Thomas à Kempis*

I lead people all over the world on adventure trips. We climb, hike, sail, raft, and do mission work across the globe. I have taken lots of people on adventure trips in dozens of countries, often in some pretty challenging environments. My team members come from all walks of life, all socioeconomic levels, and very diverse backgrounds. But I learned early on that no matter who the person is or where they're from, people can endure pretty much any challenge if they are fed well and know where they are going to sleep. So before our teams head out into the wild, I make sure that we sleep in decent accommodations and have a great meal the first night. Then I do my best to keep them well fed on the trip. No matter what challenges we face while hiking, rafting, or sailing, if those basic needs are covered, the team members can handle pretty much any challenge. When they don't get those things, the trip gets tense in a hurry.

Every human being is born with some basic needs that must be met throughout their entire lives. We all need security, connection, and control in our lives. Getting those needs met is what drives every hope and dream you have for yourself and your family. That better job, the new house, the dream marriage, the promotion, college for your kids, and padding that 401(k) retirement account are all aimed at achieving security, connection, and control.

And there's nothing wrong with you for wanting those things. Wanting them doesn't mean you're weak or incapable. It just means you're human. We were created to need those things.

In the biblical story of Adam and Eve, before they ate the forbidden fruit, they lived in a state of perfect fulfillment. God gave them everything they needed. All their needs were met.

They had security. They lived in a perfect environment with nothing to harm them.

They had perfect connection with each other and even with God Himself—so much so that God walked with them in the cool of the day.

They had tons of control. They had the run of the place. God just asked them to not do one thing: don't eat from one tree. But they fell for a lie and misused their control—and as soon as they did, the first emotion they felt was fear. The perfect security, connection, and control they had from God were replaced with fear and shame. They felt naked and vulnerable. And we've all been feeling it ever since. The story of Adam and Eve explains why we all live with the fear of not getting those three needs met. We all feel insecure and inadequate.

Never forget this: every human being feels insecure.

That pushy, loud boss of yours—insecure. He just tries to hide it with aggression and attempting to convince everyone he's right all the time.

That happy, never-discouraged friend—insecure. She just hides it with people-pleasing and humor.

Even the strongest of us feel like we aren't enough at times. At some point, we all feel like outsiders. In psychology, we call this "imposter syndrome." Try to build your self-esteem all you want, but deep down there's a voice that says we aren't what we should be. That feeling of not being enough is shame. Guilt says, "I did something wrong." Shame is deeper; it says, "There is something wrong with *me*." Deep down we know the world is not what it should be, and neither are we. And just like Adam and Eve, we feel vulnerable and afraid that our needs won't be met.

When we feel like something is threatening our security, connection, or control, it triggers emotions that help us fight off the negative feelings. And there is one emotion that promises us power in the face of feeling vulnerable.

That emotion is anger.

Anger: The Secondary Emotion

I bumped my head on the hood vent in our kitchen the other day. It hurt. Bad. My immediate reaction was to take my fist and punch the metal vent. The vent wasn't bothered—but my hand sure was. It hurt for days. My reaction of punching that metal hood vent came so quickly that I didn't have to think about it. I didn't think about what the ultimate result of my action would be. I just responded with anger.

I'm guessing you can relate. We naturally react to what's happening around us and to us. One of our most common reactions is anger or frustration.

Anger is always a secondary emotion. This means anger is a response to another emotion. Right before we feel anger, we always feel something else. Anger usually comes so quickly that we may not realize we even *felt* something else. It may only be for a split second, but there's always an emotion or threat we feel right before it. Sometimes it's a bunch of little emotions that build up over time. I'm embarrassed to say this, but the reason I went off on that hood vent was because it was the third time I had bumped my head on it that week. (That vent was constantly attacking me! We had a bumpy history.) We all have people and situations in our lives that we have enough experience with to know they are threats. Your brain remembers nearly everything, so it's constantly processing what's happening around you, looking for anything that could be a threat. It will react to anything that resembles what threatened our security, connection, or control in the past. Those reactions turn into patterns.

When I was kid, we adopted a dog named Taro. When we brought him home, we noticed that whenever we tried to pet him, he would flinch. He seemed afraid. But the weirdest thing was, sometimes Taro would go crazy and be super ferocious with certain people. I always felt sad for what he must have experienced before we adopted him that caused him to be so timid and sometimes so ferocious. Over time, with lots of love, Taro became more balanced.

We humans are way more emotionally complex than dogs, but just like Taro, we've all had experiences that stick with us and light up emotions and reactions within us. Sometimes they make us cower in fear; other times they make us attack. That's why sometimes we get angry in a conversation or situation but aren't exactly sure why. Your brain decided this situation is like a past experience that didn't go well—so it reacts with anger or frustration, trying to protect you from the negative feelings you experienced before.

There is nearly always a pattern to what triggers your anger. That pattern is what I call your anger type. Depending on your personality and past experiences, your specific anger type will be one of the following three:

1. Security-based
2. Connection-based (people with this kind of anger prefer to call it frustration)
3. Control-based

My anger is control-based. When I start feeling angry, if I slow down and consult my anger, I always find it's because something is threatening my control of a situation—which is why road traffic can transform me into a demon. Traffic doesn't bother me because I feel my security is threatened by high speeds or reckless driving. (We're going, like, seven miles per hour!) And it's not because I feel a lack of connection with the drivers in the other cars around me. I have no desire to connect with them. I just want to get where I'm going, and all the cars around me are controlling my ability to do that! Feeling helpless in traffic makes me angry.

When I get all angry in the car, it has an effect on my wife, Emily. She's much more laid back than me (thank heavens!). And she's a person with connection-based anger (frustration). The traffic doesn't make her angry, but my reaction to it does! She sees it as a threat to our connection. My insanity in traffic kills the good relational vibes she wants. To her, that traffic was an opportunity for quality time together, but I ruin the moment when I get angry. She has even threatened to walk home if I don't get it under control. Anger in me comes from threats to control. Anger in Emily comes from threats to connection. Anger is a signal that, deep inside you, something is making you feel threatened.

Anger isn't a sin. Anger is a sign.

In fact, there is such a thing as righteous anger. We *should* get angry at injustice. But even when your anger has good motives, you have to manage it correctly, or you'll just become part of the problem you're trying to confront. Righteous anger is real. But honestly, for most of us, our anger is more connected to feeling threatened. When we feel threatened, we tend to just react. But if you learn to properly manage your anger, it can actually be used as a force for good.

Anger can be a guide.

Like a road sign that gives you information about dangerous conditions ahead, anger can guide you to more self-awareness and insight.

It can help you become the person you really want to be. But to get anger working for good, you need to recognize the source of your specific anger type.

The Source

You have good reasons for your anger. You have some past experiences of not getting the security, connection, or control you needed. When negative things happen and our needs aren't met, we want to understand why. So we come up with explanations for ourselves. Sometimes those explanations give us a tainted view of the world.

If you don't get security, your tainted explanation may go something like this: *I need to protect myself. People will never do it for me. Nothing is safe. People will always abandon you.*

If you don't get connection, your tainted explanation may be this: *Who I am isn't enough. People don't value me as I am. I'm unlovable. If I don't please people, they will reject me.*

When you don't get control, your tainted explanation may go like this: *I'm not capable. I'm not in control. Nothing good lasts; it always gets taken away. I have to be perfect so I won't be embarrassed and seem like I'm out of control.*

People are complex. We all have unique personalities and lots of experiences that combine to create our interpretations of the world around us. This means the same situation can create anger in different people for different reasons. You may get angry when your children misbehave because you don't feel in control of their actions. But your spouse may see your child's behavior as personal rejection and interpret it as a lack of connection. When your boss yells at the team, it may result in embarrassment and feeling out of control for you, while another person on your team may feel a lack of security, thinking he might lose his job. You both get angry about it but for different reasons. Our personalities and past experiences make us sensitive to anything that hints at a threat to our security, connection, or control. We respond with anger to anything that threatens our area of sensitivity.

The Many Faces of Anger

Punching things, lashing out, and yelling are pretty blatant expressions of anger. But before we go any further, I want to address something important.

I work with a lot of people who genuinely believe they don't get angry. They don't yell, they don't hit things, and they even seem calm. They say they just get frustrated or irritated. I've found that people who are sensitive in the connection-based area (like Emily) prefer to call it frustration. They've seen how anger can damage connection, so they give it another name. Anger has lots of faces—including frustration. But it also shows up in lots of sneaky responses that may not seem like anger or even frustration.

Here are a few examples of subtle anger.[1]

Keeping Score: Scorekeepers don't immediately react when offended or hurt. They file the hurt away, adding offense after offense to their list. When they finally get tipped over the edge, they bring up issues from years ago—the honeymoon incident, the time you forgot to pay the electric bill, the dumb thing you said at that party—things you may never have known even bothered them. They say they aren't angry, but they've been holding a list of grievances that they remind you of when you least expect it.

Slow-Building Volcanoes: Volcanoes let anger build for a long, long time—sometimes over years or decades—until one day the person explodes. Typically, these folks hold their anger in public, and the explosion happens at home with family. Once they've erupted, they feel much better. It's all released, and they feel great. "Hey, let's all go out for pizza!" But everyone who was a victim of the explosion is

terrified, hurt, and cowering in fear—unsure when the next outburst
will happen.

Candy-Coated Razor Remarks: These folks are sweet on the
surface. They smile and put you at ease. But then subtly, they'll make
a cutting remark. One lady came up to me after a four-week series of
sermons I gave and said, "I loved this last message! God has really
been helping you improve in your speaking. You're *finally* teaching
the Bible. Great job." She smiled and walked away. *Ouch!* These folks
also love to use guilt as a tool to lash out subtly.

Shutting Down: These folks use silence and distance to express
anger. They may not talk to the person who hurt them for weeks,
even if they live in the same home. Silence is a weapon they use to
force the other person to apologize or to punish them for what
they've done. They'll act like they're trying to take the high road and
not lash out, but they're still lashing out. They're just using silence
and distance to do it.

Ganging Up: Gang fighters only express anger when surrounded
by friends. When they are in a group, they have the confidence to lash
out. A group of married couples gets together, and someone starts
bringing up problems they have with their husband or wife in front of
the group—things they never spoke out loud to their spouse. A group
around them gives them confidence in their anger.

Passive Aggression: These folks comply or agree with you to your
face, but they're devious behind your back. They gossip and undermine
you. You rarely see their anger overtly. They are subtle.

Sarcasm: Yup, sarcasm is a subtle form of anger. It just feels safer.
You can make a jab, then if people respond negatively, you can say,
"Can't you take a joke, man?"

Can you relate to any of these? They're all forms of anger. They
just appear in more socially acceptable forms than outright rage.
Again, anger is just a sign. So don't ignore the signs. When you start
feeling angry or frustrated, you need to recognize it for what it is and

then develop a strategy for how to express it in a healthy way. Anger always needs to be expressed; otherwise it just builds. But you can learn to calm the anger before it causes serious problems.

Read on—I'll show you how.

NOTE: If you weren't able to quickly identify your specific Anger Type, visit http://whyamiangry.info. It's a short online test that will help you identify the root causes of your anger.

3

Express It

Speak when you are angry and
you'll make the best speech you'll ever regret.

—*Laurence J. Peter*

I grew up in Guatemala in Central America. When I was twelve, my parents allowed me to venture out and climb my first major mountain with a few friends. It was a 12,340-foot volcano just a few miles from my home. The volcano had a strange name: Agua, which means "water" in Spanish.

We should have known problems were ahead when our local friends—the guides who knew the way—canceled on us the morning of the hike because the weather was going to get bad. But I was twelve, and the other folks hiking with me were in their early twenties, so we felt pretty invincible. We went anyway. We ended up hiking through a huge storm with no rain gear. At that altitude, it was freezing cold. A few team members got caught in a mudslide and were injured. Fortunately, a random Norwegian guy named Torgrum, whom we just happened to meet that day (I'm convinced he was some sort of Nordic guardian angel), ended up rescuing us. He carried one of our injured team members down on his back through the storm. Our water-logged experience on Agua sure made the mountain live up to its name.

But that volcano's name had nothing to do with our soaked experience hiking in the rain. The real reason the volcano got that name was because on September 10, 1541, after weeks of rain, the entire crater of the dormant volcano had filled with water and turned into a giant lake. The side of the volcano couldn't hold the pressure anymore and collapsed. A giant river of mud and water washed down the side of the volcano, destroying the city below. Crazy! An inactive volcano destroyed a city.

I think that's a pretty good picture of what happens when we don't learn to manage and express our anger. Anger doesn't just go away. If it isn't expressed, it'll just build up—like a reservoir or lake. But at some point, the pressure has to be released, and if it's out of control, it can become a destructive force.

But anger doesn't have to destroy. Just like water can be channeled and used for hydroelectric power, our anger—managed and expressed correctly—can be a powerful force that we use for good. Used correctly, anger can shift from a liability to an asset. But you have to express it correctly.

Love slows down to express anger in a healthy way.

Anger, Power, and Control

The Mandarin Chinese word for anger is *shēng qì* (pronounced *shung chee*), which translated literally means "to give birth to vital energy." Anger is a force. It's a powerful, important force. But like most powerful things, it can be used for good or bad.

Anger gives a feeling of power and control, but it actually makes the complete opposite happen. Anger makes you lose control. When anger gets triggered, your body kicks into something called Diffuse Physiological Arousal (DPA). Adrenaline surges, your muscles get tense, and you shift into fight-or-flight mode. Brain energy shifts from your prefrontal cortex (the problem-solving part of your brain) to your cortex (the "primal" part). At that point, all rational and reasonable thought basically shuts down. You go primal. You actually lose IQ points when you get angry. In that impaired state, we're prone to make some pretty impulsive decisions that we regret later.

I was a few cars back at a stoplight recently. The light turned green, but nobody moved. I patiently waited for 1.7 seconds, then I laid on my horn. *Why are we not moving?!* The guy in front of me offered a conciliatory gesture with his middle finger. I kept honking. Then I saw it—an older gentleman was rolling across the intersection as fast as he could in a wheelchair.

I came off as a total jerk. I didn't have all the facts; I just reacted. Since my anger is control-based, I reacted because I felt out of control of the situation. Laying on that horn made me feel like I was doing something—back in control—but it made me look like a jerk in the end.

I've learned the hard way that it's best to approach situations that are making us angry like a paranoid cat—cautiously, tiptoeing, with eyes wide open. Assume there is something happening behind the scenes that you don't realize. You can turn into a lion later, if needed. But if you go in roaring like a lion without all the facts, you could end up looking really foolish or causing major damage. Don't let your anger drive you to do something you'll regret once you get all the facts. Which is why when you feel yourself getting angry, the first thing you need to do is this:

1. Step away to calm down. James, the brother of Jesus, said: "Let every person be quick to hear, slow to speak, slow to anger."[1] That's a solid formula for how to control your anger—but a formula I don't follow too well. I don't know about you, but when I'm angry, I do the complete opposite. I'm slow to hear (if I listen at all), quick to speak, and quick to anger. When I feel angry or threatened, I just lash out. I don't want to hear the other person's side of things. And operating under my diminished brain capacity, I say and do things I really regret later.

Words and actions can leave a lasting impact. I still remember hurtful things people said to me when they were angry, even though it was years ago. I'm sure you do too. When we express anger in unhealthy ways, it becomes the enemy rather than our ally. So when you feel anger starting to rise up in you—the thumping in your chest, the clenched fists, the rush of heat to your forehead—force yourself to step away and give your brain time to get back to full rational capacity.

Slow down and step away. Take a deep breath and exhale as slowly as you can. Then repeat. Breathing deeply will help your body calm down.

You may need to tell the person, "I want to talk about this, but I can't right now. I need to calm down." Say it as calmly as possible. Don't just leave them hanging. Give them a reasonable time frame—in half an hour, after we put the kids to bed. Make sure they understand that you really want to do something about it and aren't just trying to ignore them. Then step away. Do whatever it takes to calm the adrenaline pumping through you. Go clean something. (That works for me. I feel soooo in control when things are clean!) Go for a run. Exercise. For our safety and yours, please don't drive! Do some physical activity to calm your body down and reset your brain.

Once you've pulled yourself out of fight-or-flight mode, the next step is to:

2. Process the issue through your anger type. Get your rational, pre-frontal cortex firing again. Remember, your anger nearly always comes from the same fear or threat. Make the connection between your anger type and what you felt was being threatened. Was it a threat to your safety or security? A threat to your connection with others or self-esteem? A threat to your control, or did you feel embarrassed? Don't just settle for knowing you're angry. Anyone can do that. Take the time to figure out *why*. If you can't figure it out on your own, pray for insight or find someone to talk through it with you. Your anger always has a deeper source. Figure out the source, and you'll be better at expressing your anger.

A well-dressed man approached me after an event where I shared this concept and asked, "Is anger *always* associated with one of those three anger types? I feel like mine isn't."

I asked, "What was the last thing that really got you angry?"

"An unexpected $400 veterinary bill," he said.

"And which anger type do you identify with most?"

"The security-based type. I grew up in poverty in Asia."

"Is it fair to say the unexpected $400 bill threatened your sense of financial security?"

He nodded. After we talked a little more, he realized most of his anger was related to anything that threatened his financial security. He made a lot of money, but his past experience of poverty made him always live in fear of not having enough. Fear of not having financial security was connected to his anger. Anything that threatened it caused him to get angry.

All of life is connected. For that guy, being forced to spend money unexpectedly was a threat to security. For other folks, that same situation could be related to connection. For others, like me, it would be more about not having control. Your anger has a specific source, and you're smart enough to figure out what's going on just below the surface—if you'll just slow down. Don't skip this step of processing what you felt was being threatened. Name it. Identify it. The next step's success depends on getting this right.

Once you identify whether it was security, connection, or control that you felt was being threatened, you'll be able to precisely express the emotion that led to the anger, improving your chances of resolving the situation.

3. Express yourself with primary emotions. Anger is always a secondary emotion, but to use anger for good, you need to express it using primary emotions. Just saying "You made me angry!" won't help resolve the situation. You need to express what you felt just before you got angry.

Our family got together recently, and during a conversation at the dinner table, I started making fun of my sister. A few minutes passed, and then she confronted me. She calmly expressed that she felt belittled by what I had said. I know it took courage and insight for her to do that. But she did it really well, and it made a huge impact. She even pointed out a bad habit I was developing. Her willingness to confront it actually helped me. When I thanked her for it, she told me that she usually doesn't realize until afterward how mad she gets about something I've said. By then it's too late to say anything, and she just leaves feeling angry and not wanting to be around me. That day she realized it quickly, processed it, and simply expressed the primary emotion she felt without anger. She told me she felt belittled—which is something I hate feeling. I could relate. I immediately apologized, and it brought us closer. She didn't allow resentment to build, and we both benefitted from her courage.

Sometimes we think that to be a loving person we just have to absorb or passively accept what bothered us and never say anything about it. We'll talk more about that in the chapter on letting things go, but for now, know that you can speak the truth about how something bothered you and still be loving and forgiving. The key is that you need to decide beforehand that you'll forgive them—even if they respond negatively when you confront them. Even if they don't respond well, you will have done the loving thing for yourself and others by expressing the emotion rather than letting it build into anger and resentment.

Properly expressing your anger is hard work. It's a lot easier to just ignore it and think you are the "bigger" person for absorbing it. Bottling it up or acting like it didn't bother you isn't the solution. The problem is that unresolved hurt and anger lead to resentment. Resentment causes serious problems down the road as we build a list of grievances against people. We'll talk more about that in a few chapters. Even worse than absorbing resentment is taking it out on other people who didn't even hurt you. If you don't properly process your anger, it will end up affecting everyone. It's like that volcano filling with water that threatens to wipe out a small city.

It can be challenging to figure out the primary emotions in the heat of your anger. You'll have to slow down and figure out the exact fear or threat you felt. Sometimes it's embarrassing to admit what was really bothering us—the primary emotion. It might take some practice and feel awkward at first. But the more you do it, the better you'll get.

Below is a chart with some primary emotion words to help you describe what you might have felt right before you got angry:

Security	Connection	Control
I felt:	I felt:	I felt:
Abandoned	Like I was being compared	Embarrassed
Vulnerable	Not good enough	Humiliated
Threatened	Belittled	Ignored
In danger	Invalidated	Helpless
Belittled	Unloved	Powerless
Alone	Rejected	Overwhelmed
Ganged up on		Belittled
		Weak

Once you've nailed down that primary emotion, express it very carefully. Remember, anger is *your* problem. So keep it about *your* issues. Don't blame. If we aren't careful, our words can sound like we're accusing someone of doing it intentionally, which usually isn't the case. In general, people are good-willed. They aren't trying to make you angry. In fact, most of the time they don't even know they upset you. Assume the best.

Simply state—without accusing—how the situation made you feel. Use "I" statements rather than "you" statements. I find this line to be helpful when expressing my feelings: "When I found out _____, it made me feel _____."

Here are some examples:

"When I found out I had been left out of that meeting, I felt overlooked, like my ideas didn't matter."

"In our conversation, all I could hear was the tone used, and it made me feel belittled."

"When my shift was changed without telling me, it made me feel helpless."

"When I see how our money is being spent, it makes me feel unsafe. I worry we won't have enough when we need it."

This takes practice. But trust me, you can do this. For the record, if you are married or in a relationship, you *really* need this. It can save your relationship. If you're dealing with a young child, you may not be able to resolve the issue through clearly communicating your emotions. You may just have to talk it out with a friend or process it on your own. But the process of figuring out what is really triggering the anger will be helpful in guiding your child through their own emotions as they get older. Know yourself so you can help your kids do the same thing.

When you express your anger using primary emotions in a calm way, you'll find that people can relate and are usually pretty understanding. We all know what it's like to feel those primary emotions of feeling abandoned, rejected, or embarrassed. Sure, there are some people who will intentionally provoke you. But most people don't even realize it when they're making you angry. Again, assume the best about people. Go in like a cat, not a roaring lion. When you express the deeper feeling that led to your anger, you'll be amazed how people respond. And the anger won't keep building inside you.

Can you imagine what could change in your relationships and inside yourself if you learned to really express what was bothering you? Instead of allowing anger to cause separation, expressing your feelings could actually draw you closer together. You wouldn't have all that resentment building up inside you, causing you to avoid certain people, and making you lose sleep. Learning to express your feelings correctly can turn frustration and anger from a liability into an asset. An asset that makes you more self-aware and strengthens your relationships.

And this is where things get really good.

Once you've processed and expressed your anger, it's time to unlock the insight that anger has to offer. It's time to consult your anger and let it show you where you've been limiting yourself and living out of fear, anxiety, and hurry instead of love.

4

Consult Your Anger

The longer you listen, the more you will learn,
the less angry you will become.

—*Andy Stanley*

The first Summit Leaders trip I ever led was a twenty-eight-mile trek through the Andes Mountains in Peru where we hiked to the ancient Inca fortress of Machu Picchu. It's a really challenging hike through rain forests, over high mountain passes, and deep into lush green valleys. It was my first time to ever do a trip like this, and I had a nationally known Christian leader as the speaker for the hike. I wanted to make it the trip of a lifetime for him and the team. I was trying to control and manage everything so nothing would go wrong.

But just two months before the trip, torrential rains caused floods that washed out the roads and main train lines to Machu Picchu. This made getting the team to and from the trail really complicated and confusing. The outfitter made some mistakes with food and tents. We got delayed because of transportation issues related to the messed-up train lines. My control-based anger was triggered the entire trip! I was on overdrive. I couldn't enjoy it because I was so obsessed with making everything go just like I wanted it to—but it didn't. It was a huge relief when every team member made it to Machu Picchu, in spite of the problems, and we boarded our train back to Cusco. Everyone agreed the trip was a huge success.

On the train ride back from Machu Picchu, a guy on the team started showing some pictures of amazing orchids and tropical birds to the people sitting around him. I scooted closer to look at the little screen. "Wow. That's amazing. Where did you shoot all those pictures?" I asked.

He gave me a perplexed look. "These are all pictures from the trail we just hiked, bro."

I almost didn't believe him. I hadn't seen any of it. I was so laser-focused that I missed some of the best parts of that trip because I was in a state of perpetual anger, trying to control everything. Anger tends to give you tunnel vision, which means you miss out on a lot of things happening around you. No matter how good things may be around you, if you're angry (or anxious), you probably won't see it. But once you've learned to control your anger, you can step away from it and give it a closer look. You can pay attention to what's really happening with a clear mind. And paying attention is a really, really important expression of love.

We pay attention to what we really love. If you love plants, you'll watch to make sure they're getting enough water, fertilizer, and sun. If you love your car, you'll do regular maintenance, maybe even upgrades. If you love your marriage and your kids, you'll do the same. If you love yourself (which you should—after all, God does), then you'll pay attention to the deeper parts of you that are affected when you feel angry or frustrated. When you slow down to pay attention, you'll start to unlock the insight that your anger can offer. You'll start to see how to fix things in your life.

When a company or organization feels stuck or isn't seeing the growth it wants, it will often bring in an outside consultant that can view things with different eyes and show it a way forward. We're too close to our lives to see clearly, so consultants pay attention to things we've overlooked or ignored. They bring it to the surface. Believe it or not, you have a great consultant for your own personal growth and path forward. That consultant is anger. When you consult your anger, it can show you areas of your life where you are living short of all God has for you.

Love slows down to consult your anger.

Where It All Started

When I was a kid, I went to a strict religious school. One particular teacher in third grade knew how to use embarrassment and shame as a weapon to get me to behave. That's the first time I remember my control-based anger showing up. That teacher made me furious on a regular basis. One time, he wrote a note to my mom in which he accused me of doing something I didn't do. He followed me out to our car to make sure I gave her the note. In front of him and my mom, I tore up the note and threw it at him. That angry response led to the worst spanking of my life. The spanking obviously didn't work, because I'm still proud of standing up to that punk teacher! I'd do it all over again!

That experience was just the start of my control-based anger. On top of that, my dad was a pastor, and I lived under constant scrutiny. I'll never forget a lady telling me I had "grieved the Holy Spirit" because I was running in church. She embarrassed me in front of everyone there when she rebuked me. My experience of being a pastor's kid, combined with the harsh treatment from that teacher, left me sensitive in that area. I'm hyper-sensitive to anyone or anything that threatens to control or embarrass me.

Analyze your anger for a moment. What or whom makes you angry on a regular basis? Traffic? Your mother-in-law? Your kids not eating? Don't condemn yourself or say it shouldn't make you angry or frustrated. The fact is, it does.

When the psalmist wrote, "Be angry, and do not sin; ponder in your own hearts on your beds, and be silent,"[1] he was talking about the power of consulting your anger. When you get angry, don't just react and risk doing something you regret—evaluate what's happening. Ponder. Slow down. Pay attention to your thoughts and emotions. When you evaluate what's really happening, your anger and frustration can show you a lot about what's going on in your mind and heart. Your anger is telling you something. It's showing you an area of your life where you aren't operating at full capacity.

Heading It Off at the Pass

A good consultant always gives the people they are consulting some action steps to help resolve the issues they've identified. We need to do the same with the insight we get from our anger. We need to identify what gets our anger going and develop a plan to get it under control. Your plan will be specific to your anger type and life situation.

I've had to do this in my own life. When I know I'm going into a situation where someone else might have control over my time or movement, I have to mentally prepare myself. If I know I'm going to hit traffic (and Emily won't be in the car looking for quality time), I have an audiobook cued up. When I'm going to the doctor, I clear my entire schedule for the day and that evening. (Not really, but sometimes it feels like I should!) When I've been paying attention to my anger and know what situations in the past got me angry, I'm much less prone to getting irritated. You'll need to do the same. If being around certain people or situations is unavoidable, go in mentally and emotionally prepared with a plan.

There are probably certain routines that, based on your anger type, make you more prone to anger. Things like getting kids ready for school in the morning, trying to get your three-year-old to stay at the table and eat dinner, and getting everyone to church on time on Sunday morning all have a pattern and specific time connected to them. When you get too hungry, you are more likely to get angry. For some, angry arguments related to money always happen at the end of the month when finances are tight. Recognize the patterns so you can head it off at the pass.

My wife always gives me a pep talk when she knows we'll be driving through rush-hour traffic. She'll pull me aside, place one hand on each shoulder, and look me straight in the eye. "Joël, it's 5 p.m. Traffic is going to be bad. This is life. You are going to be OK. Stay calm." Silly as it may seem, that little reminder helps me prepare. You may need to give yourself your own pep talk or come up with creative ways to keep your anger in check too. Have the kids lay out their clothes in the morning. Eat a snack to calm your hunger, then feed the kids so you'll have patience with them. Put a shock collar on your teenager who refuses to wake up. (Just kidding—but hmm...)

There are usually seasons or times of year when we feel more angry or frustrated. Hospitals see a huge increase in admissions for behavioral issues at the end of summer. Studies have shown that anger and violence actually increase during the hotter months.[2] I travel all over the world, but I live in central Texas, where the month of August is basically the seventh level of Hell. I don't like the heat. (I also don't like cold. Yes, I have issues.) But I can't control the weather, so I tend to get really angry in late summer. August is also when my daughter goes to school, which means we are bleeding money the entire month. High electric bills, school supplies, registration fees, and other random bills all appear on the countertop. I see unexpected charges on the credit card. The heat combined with all the money I'm spending gets me pretty irritated. For years, August was a tense time around our house. To combat this, I've started setting aside money for August and spending lots of time in the water to keep me sane.

For some, Christmas and other major holidays lead to anger. Being around family. Kids out of school. Traffic and all the hustle and bustle. Sometimes it's anger combined with sadness, missing a loved one who is no longer there. For others, it's the stress of being back with family members who have a history of hurting us. (You moved away for a reason, right?) Seasons have a definite impact on our patterns of anger.

Speaking of seasons, know what causes lots of anger? Change. Even those of us who say we like change only really like it on our terms. Change leaves us feeling uncertain and confused. We like to know what to expect, but change shakes all that up. A few months after I got hired by a Fortune 500 company, they sent all of their employees a book about embracing change. I was young and new at the company. I hadn't developed any routines or systems in my work. Sending that book seemed like a waste of money. Shortly after that, they announced they'd be transitioning to an entirely new computer system. We would all have to be retrained. For folks who had been at the company for twenty-plus years, that was the final straw. Some of them actually took early retirement and left, angry at the company and complaining that management was trying to force them out—all over change. But the older I get, the more I understand. Change is uncomfortable. It brings lots of uncertainty and feels like a threat.

If you are going through a life transition, be prepared to consult your anger on a regular basis. It will be giving you lots of insight. If you've recently moved to a new city or house, started a new job, had a baby or adopted a child, had a major change in your financial situation, or lost a loved one, don't be surprised if you struggle with anger. Anger is part of the cycle of grieving. Those changes have a major impact on us and threaten our security, connection, and control. We don't know what to expect anymore. That leads to fear, uncertainty, and anger. If you're in a transition, you may need to adjust some expectations (we'll talk more about that a few chapters from now) or reevaluate some systems and values you hold. But know this: if you'll recognize the source and patterns of your anger, you'll get it under control and get some serious self-awareness through it.

Keep Track of It

So here's a suggestion: start tracking your anger. Make an anger journal. Take it with you in your pocket or purse. When you feel yourself getting angry (or even mildly frustrated), pay attention to what's happening. Write down what happened, when it was, and who was involved. Here's an example:

TIME	LOCATION	PEOPLE INVOLVED	WHAT HAPPENED?
7:45 a.m.	On the road	Other drivers	I'm going to be late because of traffic

Traffic was the issue. Now, identify if it was about a threat to security, connection, or control.

Here's another example:

TIME	LOCATION	PEOPLE INVOLVED	WHAT HAPPENED?
10:11 a.m.	Office	My boss and Gina	They met without me and didn't consider my ideas

What's the issue here? Well, it seems like a relational issue—a threat to connection with others or self-esteem. It may take a little while to figure out exactly which of the big three was being threatened, but if you'll pay attention, I'm certain you'll figure it out. If you need to, talk to someone about it and let them help you process it.

Keep track of your anger for a week or two. You'll see a pattern. It'll also make your specific anger type really clear. While you read this book, you may find yourself remembering a few more instances from your past that made you really angry. Write those down too. Understand what consistently makes you angry. Know the patterns. Then you can begin to consult your anger for the insight it can bring.

Consult Your Anger

When we decided to buy our first home, we looked for months and finally found a place that was perfect. I was ready to buy the place, but my dad highly recommended that we hire an inspector to look at it first. I couldn't imagine what the inspector could find that I couldn't see on my own, but I trusted my dad, so I got an inspection. A few days later, we received a multiple-page report pointing out every tiny flaw in the home. Talk about discouraging! At first glance, the report made it seem like the house was on the verge of falling apart. But the truth was, it wasn't. There were just some issues we needed to be aware of. And I'm glad we were. We went in with eyes wide open after the report. That inspector pointed out potential problems where I didn't have the knowledge to realize one existed. That's what you pay an inspector to do—consult with you about problems. Based on his expert feedback, you can move forward with wisdom and confidence.

Just like that inspector, anger can be your greatest expert consultant. It can help you inspect areas of your life that you've pushed down or simply avoided facing. It brings them to your attention so you can address them. It can make you aware of potential problems deep in the framework of who you are that you may have not even realized were there. Sometimes those deep issues are limiting you and your potential without you even knowing it. Anger is always pointing us to greater insights about ourselves. Just like that home-inspection report, what your anger reveals might make you really uncomfortable. It might even discourage you. You may feel like a real fixer-upper. It may mean some work on parts of you that you've been overlooking. But trust me—the work will be worth it. Facing the truth will always set you free.

That first house I bought had tons of potential, but it needed a little renovation first. You have loads of potential sitting inside you that you can't even see. If you'll consult your anger and put in the work to fix it, it will pull out parts of you—really amazing parts—that you didn't even realize were there. They've just been hiding behind your anger and fear. But you'll only realize that potential when you choose to manage and consult your anger and fear.

Anger always points to fear. Anxiety, worry, and fear will always shrink your world and limit you. The life you really want—the life God has for you—is usually on the other side of facing your greatest fears. Anger reveals what those are. When you identify the fear, you can attack it with love. Love drives out fear.

And that's what the next section is about—facing and conquering fear and anxiety.

PART II

Face Your Fear

5

Face Your Fear

There is no fear in love.
But perfect love drives out fear....
The one who fears is not made perfect in love.

—*1 John 4:18*

I am terrified of heights.

I don't even like walking over bridges that have those grates you can see through. It makes me panic, and I run as fast as I can across the bridge. People don't believe me when I admit my fear of heights. They say, "But you climb all those mountains and stuff."

My response: "Yeah, but I stay close to the mountain and never look over the edge while I'm climbing."

Which is how I've managed to stay alive. I've learned that it's OK to acknowledge my fear. Ignoring or denying your fear is just lying to yourself. I have to acknowledge it, but I refuse to let it keep me from moving ahead. Healthy fear is a good thing. It can keep us out of trouble and danger. But fear is unhealthy when it consumes our thoughts and makes us run faster or freezes us in our tracks. That kind of fear limits us and keeps us from truly walking in love. We can't let fear control us.

Fear is a natural human reaction. It's the first emotion Adam and Eve felt when they realized they were naked. We've all felt fear ever since. It shows up in our lives as worry, anxiety, nervousness, concern, and anger. Anger and fear are directly connected. Threats to our security, connection, or control create fear and then lead to anger. Nothing can limit you quite like fear. It has a way of shrinking your world and causing you to live in a state of constant vigilance. You can't be present to enjoy what's around you when you are afraid. If you're always worried and anxious, there's no possible way you can really give and receive love—you'll be too preoccupied with protecting yourself. There is no fear in love. The good news is that real love drives out fear. But first, you have to be willing to recognize and face what has been driving your fear.

Love slows down to face your fears.

The Faces of Fear

I've struggled with major fear my entire life. When I was ten, I read a book about the end of the world that was totally not age-appropriate. At that moment, fear showed up at the doorstep of my life and has been trying to get in ever since. I've been afraid of dying, afraid of what would happen to my family if I died, afraid of family members getting sick, and afraid of not reaching my goals. And that list is just what I was afraid of yesterday! I can always find things to be anxious or worried about. When my daughter came along, the fear reached new levels. Fear has been a constant companion. Which, I now realize, is why I've struggled with anger all my life. To beat the anger, I always have to address the fear.

We live in a world driven by fear. Fear puts us into fight-or-flight mode. It drives us to action. So marketers, politicians, and the media love to use it to catch our attention and get us to buy or vote or act. With more access to knowledge and information than ever before in history, we have a constant stream of information about what we should be afraid of coming our way. Fear sells. And we buy it. When

I start talking about fear online or at church, I get lots of responses from people who are living under crushing fear and anxiety. Many statistics, and just a basic look around us, show that anxiety is at an all-time high.

Fear looks different for every person. It doesn't always show up as worry or anxiety or trying to avoid spiders or snakes; it has lots of faces. Here are a few common forms of fear I've seen as I've worked with people over the years:

1. Nameless Anxiety: This is what my fear tends to look like. It's just an overwhelming feeling that something bad is about to happen. Life can be going great, but you wake up with a sense of dread. Impending doom! (Say that with a deep voice and lots of echo; that's how it sounds in my head.) Maybe it was my upbringing in religious schools, but for many years I projected this fear onto God. I was just certain that He was waiting around the corner to pummel me for not being all I should be.

2. Indecision: I work with lots of people who are frustrated because they don't know what they really want in life. They have a hard time making decisions—little and big. They can't commit to anything. Most of the time, after sorting through it with them, we find that fear is driving the indecision. They're afraid that if they make a choice it will be the wrong one. They don't want to define what they really want because they might never get it. Then they'd be even more disappointed and frustrated with themselves.

3. Catastrophizing: I struggle with this one too. Something out of the ordinary happens, and my brain takes off to the worst possible scenario. New neighbors move in and make tons of noise during the move, and I'm certain they are going to be horrible neighbors. A small spot appears on my arm, and I'm sure I'm going to die of skin cancer. The candidate I voted against wins the election, and I'm sure we'll soon be living under a tyrannical dictatorship. Taking one small thing and turning it into a catastrophe in your mind is a form of fear.

4. Checking Out/Apathy: I work with lots of people who deal with fear by checking out when things get difficult or overwhelming. They feel helpless or incapable of making any difference in their situation, so they find ways to numb or distract themselves from confronting their anxiety and fear. Over the long term, this denial can lead to just saying, "What does it really matter anyway?"

I've seen lots of leaders get overwhelmed by hard choices. Rather than face the challenges, they pour their energy into all sorts of other activities. In the meantime, those looking to them for decisive leadership become afraid and angry. Apathy and checking out can be expressions of fear.

Fear also shows up in the questions we quietly think or ask ourselves:

What if my best days are behind me?

What if I can't give my kids a better life than my parents gave me?

What if my race rejects me for doing this? People of my color don't do this kind of thing.

What if I'm not enough? What if I don't have what it takes to do this?

What if I try and fail? Will I ever get back what I gave up?

What if I never achieve my dreams, and this is as good as it gets?

What if our marriage never gets better?

What's frustrating is that fear isn't necessarily rational. Sometimes our fear and worry make sense. But a lot of the time, fear is downright irrational. The worst part is that we may know it's irrational, but we can't rationally talk ourselves out of it. If you've struggled with major fear and worry, you know what I'm talking about. It consumes your thoughts. And the more we try to push it down, the bigger it gets.

Fear grows in the dark. It makes you feel isolated and alone. That's why the best thing we can do is identify and name our fear—and then face it. Something powerful happens when you're able to admit and say what you're really afraid of. When fear is brought out of the darkness and into the light, it starts to lose its power.

Slow Down, Don't Drown

Not long after my sister got her driver's license, she was driving through a downpour and found herself in a flooded intersection. The water was rising fast around her car. She got scared and made an impulsive decision. She slammed her foot on the gas pedal and surged forward. Water shot up into the engine and stalled her car. Fortunately, she was able to wade to safety, but it took weeks of costly repairs to overhaul that vehicle. There are signs all over our town in low-lying areas, warning you to drive slowly through high water. They say: "Slow Down, Don't Drown."

At one point, my dad asked her, "What made you decide to floor it?"

Her answer was pretty insightful. "Well, I was scared and knew I was in trouble. So I figured the faster I went, the quicker I'd be out of it."

That makes pretty good sense. And that's how most of us live our lives. There's no problem that can't be solved if you just go faster! But that doesn't work when the waters are rising. When life gets stressful and we start to feel worried, anxious, and overwhelmed, the answer is not to go faster. You have to proceed slowly and cautiously.

When our brains shift into fight-or-flight mode, we do whatever it takes to eliminate the fear. For most of us, this means flight. We run away from the fear, going faster and faster. We avoid and deny. We run to anything that promises security, connection, or control. But all that running can have some disastrous results.

We have to make a conscious decision to slow down, face our fears, and process them. All of them—the taxes you never filed, adding up how much debt you actually have, the growing concerns with your spouse's behavior. The fears we don't face get bigger. They grow in the darkness of denial or when we refuse to talk about them. They get stronger. They steal your peace of mind. They make you lose sleep. But when we start to recognize fear for what it is—in all its many faces—we can learn to move forward in spite of it. When you slow down and wade through the dark waters of what you fear the most, something amazing happens. Often, the simple act of naming your fear and facing off with it causes it to lose its stranglehold on you.

Fear will never completely go away. It will always be present, but it doesn't have to control or limit you. The goal isn't to be fearless. The goal is to fear less. God hasn't given a spirit of fear, but of power and love and a sound mind.

Driving out Fear

Your anger type—security-based, connection-based, control-based— could just as well be called your fear type. Each anger type has some specific fears attached to it.

Security-based fear is related to anything that threatens your physical, emotional, or financial safety.

Connection-based fear is usually related to concerns about feeling rejected, not valued, or not being heard, seen, or validated.

Control-based fear is related to anything that threatens your empowerment or autonomy or is something which has the potential to embarrass or humiliate you.

I took the Enneagram personality assessment recently. I'm a Type Eight. It said one of my greatest fears is being controlled. *Nailed it!* I'm always asking if something will control me or has the potential to embarrass me. The embarrassment thing is a real problem, because when you start something new, you always run the risk of it not working. I've launched lots of new things, but every time I do, I still get worried that I'll be embarrassed or fail. I have to press through the fear. You'll have to do the same thing. You have to constantly evaluate the choices you are making and make sure they aren't being driven by fear. Choices driven by fear never lead to love.

At an event where I spoke recently, a man shared that he realized fear was messing up his second marriage. He had been through a messy divorce that left him penniless and struggling. He got remarried, but in the back of his mind, he was always afraid that his new wife would leave. He kept their finances and assets separate. Needless to say, this created some serious insecurity in his new wife. She had begun to pull away and was hiding some of her own money, thinking he wasn't really committed to the marriage. His fear of another divorce caused him to take preemptive measures that ended up pushing him toward the thing he feared the most—another divorce.

When we get focused on our fear, it shrinks our world. When you get consumed with all the what-ifs of everything that could go wrong, you can't even think about the what-ifs of all that could go right. Focusing on the good what-ifs is what faith is all about.

Which brings us to the really, really good news: If you live with lots of anxiety and fear, it means you have the potential to live with some serious faith. Fear and faith aren't opposites. Fear is actually a form of faith; it's just faith in the wrong thing. A fearful person is just a faithful person who believes bad things will happen—not good things. Faith is believing in God's promises and goodness. What's amazing is that God says all you need is a tiny amount of faith—the size of a mustard seed. Start small. You don't have to drum up loads of faith. You just have to take a small step. When you step out and face your fear, little by little, God sustains you, and it builds your faith. You replace your fear with confidence (faith) in God's love.

Love drives out fear.

And "drives" is the key word here.

You can't sit around and wait for the fear to magically go away before you face it. It won't. The fear will just get bigger. You have to voluntarily move toward your fear. Do it slowly, but keep moving. Face the thing you fear in small doses. Like a vaccine that gives your body a small amount of a disease so you can build resistance, you fight off fear by exposing yourself to small doses of what you fear. The fear will still be there, but little by little, it will lose its power over you.

In the words of Joseph Campbell: "The cave you fear to enter holds the treasure that you seek." Faith is only really exercised in darkness and uncertainty. If you can see the outcome and the road is clear, then you don't need faith. Faith means moving ahead into the darkness. The life you really want is just on the other side of what you fear. Use wisdom but take small steps toward your fear. Small steps are the essence of faith.

Fear never goes away completely. Just do it afraid.

Face the Fear

What would your life look like if you weren't afraid? What could you do differently if you feared and worried less? Is it possible that at least some of your deepest anger and frustration occurs because you've been living in fear of failure, or not being enough, or not having what it takes?

Here's a bigger question: What happened in your life that made you so afraid in this area? You have your reasons. And they probably make a lot of sense to you. But if they're limiting and frustrating you, it may be time to get to the root of that issue and undo its power.

Our greatest fears typically come from past disappointments. We all have disappointments and unmet hopes and dreams. So in the next chapter, we're gonna talk about where our fears came from and how to drive them out with love knowing that God has not given us a spirit of fear but of power, and love, and self-discipline.[1]

6

Face Your Disappointment

If I am to meet with a disappointment,
the sooner I know it,
the more of life I shall have to wear it off.

—*Thomas Jefferson*

The church softball league my dad and I played in for a few years included a team that probably shouldn't have been there. They were all hyper-competitive, loved to talk trash, and used tons of profanity on the field. They called themselves by a vague, Christiany name: Brothers in Christ.

I'd regularly single one or two of them out and ask, "What church are you from?"

They'd respond by looking at the ground and mumbling, "Uh ... a small church across town." They could never name the pastor or exactly where the church was.

My dad and I concluded it was a group of guys who wanted to be able to dominate and win, so they picked a church league to play in. One day, we showed up, and all the games were canceled because there had been a bench-clearing brawl on the field ... in our church league. Guess which team started the fight?

Lots of the guys on that team reminded me of Uncle Rico from the movie *Napoleon Dynamite*, all trying to relive their glory days of high school sports. "If coach would have just put me in during the fourth quarter of that last game, I could have gone pro. I'd be with my soulmate!" Off the field, all those softball players were functioning members of society. Some were even successful businessmen. But I tend to believe they had some unresolved anger and disappointment about their lives. Life hadn't turned out as they expected, so they played sports in an angry and aggressive way.

Disappointment from the past can easily turn into anger in the present. Life never turns out quite how we envisioned it. For many of us, it falls way short of an ideal we had. We look around and think: *It wasn't supposed to be this way.* We were supposed to be married or retired or financially strong by now. But life threw a curveball. It's easy to get cynical and angry. And then that disappointment has a tendency to creep into even the most innocuous of parts of our lives— like softball or social media posts. We start ruining the fun for everyone, and we end up isolated and alone.

The older we get, the more disappointments we face—missed opportunities, chances we never took, failed relationships, and dreams that never became reality. We came into our marriages, careers, and ministries with some high expectations. Lots of times those expectations were based on something we saw on TV or read in a book. We had dreams of security, connection, and control, but instead we got disappointment. And we're afraid of being disappointed again. That disappointment drives our fear and anxiety. To release anger and fear, we have to acknowledge and face our disappointments at some point.

Love slows down to face our disappointments.

Dangerous Disappointment

A few years ago, I got really interested in a not-for-profit organization that was doing work in Africa. It was a great organization, and I followed it for several years. But I noticed some of its material was becoming increasingly angry that no one seemed to care about the plight of the people the organization was helping. A few years later, I heard a story in the news about the founder of that organization having a mental breakdown and creating a big, shameful scene in public. A friend of mine who was really close to that leader was there when it all happened. He told me the founder had become obsessed with righting the injustice he saw—which really was horrible—but was angry that no one seemed to care as much as he did. His disappointment and anger with those he was trying to mobilize to fix the problem caused him to snap. When we have expectations and hopes that don't happen as quickly as we want—or not at all—they can easily turn into frustration and anger.

When we're disappointed, we tend toward one of two extreme responses. Some folks give up and say, "It's hopeless." They get cynical and jaded that life isn't what they think it should be. Sometimes these folks just decide to check out of life. They numb their disappointment with alcohol, drugs, entertainment, or anything else that will distract them from the fact that they don't like how things turned out.

The other extreme is folks who shift their disappointment into what they believe to be righteous anger. They take on good causes, but their efforts are tainted with unhealthy anger and resentment. Often the injustice they're trying to confront is a response to their own personal past hurt. They know the pain and are seeking to right an injustice. Their motives are good, but they use anger that wasn't consulted to fuel their rage. It's reckless and uncontrolled anger. They feel righteous for fighting the government, or church, or some particular group they believe is oppressing the world. The work they are doing to fight injustice is good, but it's tainted by bitterness. If the bitterness grows, it shifts into just wanting the world to burn.

Don't get me wrong—we absolutely need to fight injustice. But you don't drive out injustice with bitterness. You have to drive it out with love. And you can't love when you're working from disappointment, fear, and anger. That's why Jesus talked about removing the log from your own eye first. We need to recognize our disappointment and wrestle with it inside us rather than project it on the world. If we don't, it will build into something unhealthy and potentially dangerous. Replace your hurt and disappointment with love first—remove the log that's blocking you—then when you see clearly, you can truly confront issues in the world from a place of love rather than anger and bitterness.

The Face of Disappointment

We all have expectations about what life should or could look like. We may not sit around thinking about those expectations, but deep inside we all have ideas about what our finances, careers, and relationships should look like. When those expectations aren't met, they lead to disappointment. Before my daughter was born, I would watch someone else's child have a meltdown and think, *My kids will never do that. I'll keep them under control.* I'll never forget being on a flight to New York and realizing, *We are that family.* The ones with the screaming child we couldn't control. Nothing can shatter your expectations like the realities that come with parenting. You love your kids, but it's nothing like you imagined. The disappointment may have started when you found out it was a girl, or a boy, or twins, or maybe your child was born with a disability. That seed of disappointment starts to grow if it isn't addressed. Before we realize it, our disappointment can lead to resentment toward our spouse, kids, jobs, or even God.

Recently, a lady shared with me how disappointed she was about her marriage. When she was young, she married a man who didn't share her faith. She was certain that once she got married her husband would convert to her belief system. He never did. She said she harbored anger and resentment toward her husband for twenty-plus years. But then she realized her issue was really with God. She had an expectation—a hope—in her mind, and God hadn't done a miracle to bring about her ideal. She said that when she finally admitted her disappointment with God, for the first time in her life, she felt peace about her marriage. Sure, she still hopes her husband will have a change of heart, but she's not angry anymore—which means, possibly for the first time, that she can actually love him just as he is.

If you've ever hoped for God to act in a certain way—bring healing, fix a situation—you've probably been disappointed. God is always dependable, but He is rarely predictable. When He doesn't live up to our expectations, it's only natural to feel disappointed. I know the idea of being disappointed with God makes some people uncomfortable. Are we allowed to be disappointed with God? Does God owe us an explanation? Those are great questions that I'll leave to the theologians to debate. Whether it's right or wrong, the feeling of disappointment is real, and you have to acknowledge it. Otherwise, you can be sure it's limiting your ability to love God and others. You can only push it down or ignore it for so long before it shows up as anxiety, anger, and resentment. The good news is that you aren't the first one to be disillusioned with God's ways. In fact, disappointment with God happens to the best of us.

John the Baptist was one of the first to recognize that Jesus would change the world. He actually got to see Heaven open and heard a voice announcing who Jesus was. Things were looking up for the world—the Savior was here! But shortly after that epic moment, John was unjustly arrested and thrown into prison. I'm sure he expected that any day Jesus would come to the rescue. God, in the flesh, was just a few miles away. Surely he would deliver John, right? But He never came. So John sent some disciples to ask Jesus, "Are you the one … or should we be looking for another?" Clearly, Jesus hadn't met John's expectations. The crazy thing is, Jesus didn't really answer John's questions. He just did a bunch of miracles and told John's disciples to tell John what they had seen. Then Jesus said, "and blessed is the one who is not offended by me."[1]

I'm gonna make a bold statement here. If you've never been disappointed, it's possible that you've never had real faith in God. Maybe your faith was in the tiny box you wanted God to fit in. Big faith and disappointment will always go hand in hand. Being disappointed just means you had faith, which is a good thing. When you really believe God is going to come through and He doesn't respond how you expected, it will lead to disappointment at some point. God rarely works exactly how we think He should. His perspective is bigger than ours. He sees it all.

Sometimes we get so laser-focused on our expectations of what life should look like that we actually become narrow-minded. As a kid, I used to take empty toilet paper rolls and pretend they were binoculars. It didn't help me see better; in fact, it actually limited what I could see. I'd trip over things that were right in front of me because my perspective was limited. We all do this in life sometimes. It's really easy to get a very narrow perspective on what we think life should look like. I get narrow-minded about timelines of when things should happen. If it doesn't happen right when I think is best, I get frustrated and anxious. I'm certain my life is wasting away and that my best years are behind me. I get narrow-minded about which resources I think I need to accomplish what I feel called to do. When I don't have what I think I need, I'm prone to blame circumstances and feel sorry for myself. Like walking around with toilet paper rolls on our eyes, we want everything to cram into that narrow view of the world. We have expectations for our kids, our finances, our marriages, and our futures that we think should fit into those rolls—or roles. But life isn't that simple. And we can end up missing the big picture. God feels no need to fit into our narrow worldview. (And if He could, we'd be in big trouble!) When those rolls are over our eyes, we can't even see ourselves clearly. If we aren't willing to open up our narrow perspective, we will become increasingly frustrated.

I think that's the essence of Jesus's response to John the Baptist. He wanted John to broaden his perspective beyond his personal expectations and see that something bigger was in the works. He essentially told John that a blessing comes when we're disappointed but choose to not be offended at how God decides to do things. The same is true in our lives. God is working on something really, really big in the world and, more specifically, in your life. You may not see it, but you can be confident that even when you feel disappointed, He's at work. His plan for your life is what you would want your plan to be if you knew all the details.

Wrestling with God

It's OK to wrestle with disappointment with God. It's OK to admit your frustration. He can take it. But always be willing to take the toilet paper rolls of expectations off your eyes. Those rolls will just lead to anger and frustration. When we admit our disappointment with God and then surrender to reality, it keeps disappointment from turning into resentment and anger.

The name *Israel* means "wrestles with God." Is it possible that God actually *wants* us to wrestle with Him? I can't help but wonder if wrestling with our negative feelings toward God and His ways can actually strengthen our love for Him. Our greatest emotional wrestling matches tend to be with those we love most; should God be any exception? Obviously, we do it with reverence for who He is, but I think we miss out on an important element of growth in our relationship with God when we aren't willing to acknowledge our disappointment with Him and His ways.[2]

In the wise words of Joseph Campbell, "You must give up the life you planned in order to have the life that is waiting for you." Life may not have turned out like you had hoped, but trust me on this: God is in full control.

Face your disappointment about your marriage, your career, your kids. Don't ignore the reality that life isn't what you had hoped.

Ignoring it just leads to anxiety and anger. Admit the hurt when you have expectations that aren't met. Admit you had an ideal that wasn't met. Wrestle with God a little. Then release it.

What would your life look like if you actually decided to let go of your disappointment and appreciate the life you have, right now? No, life is not what you expected. But it is what it is. Once you face what it is, you can stop living in constant fear of being disappointed. You can stop being tyrannized by your own expectations. You can decide that you'll move forward without fear knowing that God will ultimately work all things together for your good. You can let go of your expectations and be grateful for what you have right now. It's not over. God often uses your greatest disappointments to lead you to your destiny. He still has a plan, and no matter what has happened to you in your past, He can accomplish His work in you. The best news is this: once we've come to grips with our disappointment, we can face it and reframe it to begin to see our lives from a completely new framework.

7

Reframe It

When we are no longer able to change a situation,
we are challenged to change ourselves.

—*Viktor Frankl*

When I heard that my college pastor was going to climb Mount Kilimanjaro, the highest mountain in Africa, for some reason it sounded like a good idea. So I told him I wanted to go with him. I worked extra hours and saved every penny to afford the trip. I trained hard. I was in the best shape of my life. I took the physical preparation seriously, but I hadn't done much research on what happens to your body when you climb a mountain that big. I paid the price for that ignorance. I got seriously ill with acute mountain sickness (AMS) and had to rush back down to a lower altitude. I spent all that money and put in all that time training, but I had to bail out before I made it to the top. I'll never forget that night of hiking in the pitch-black darkness, emptying the contents of my stomach and dry heaving every few steps—the weakest I'd ever felt. I remember thinking, *What on earth was I thinking doing this?*

For years, failing to get to the top of that mountain haunted me. When people would ask about my experience on Kili, I always got insecure and tried to steer the conversation in another direction. I had no desire to revisit my failure. Ten years later, I finally made it to the top of Kilimanjaro, but fortunately, I had come to grips with my failure first. I realized *I* wasn't a failure. I had just failed to make it to the top of one mountain. My failure didn't define me. And neither does yours.

Your past doesn't define you. Neither do your current circumstances.

In fact, if you learn to see your past correctly, you'll see that it has prepared you for where you are now. I needed that experience. My natural tendency is to get irritated with people who aren't physically prepared when they go on a hike with me. Had I not failed on Kili, I doubt I would have been able to have any compassion for people on my teams who were struggling. To be a better leader, I needed to fail. Which means it really wasn't a failure. It was preparation. But to get to that place, I needed a shift in perspective. I needed a new interpretation of the experience. Often the only thing that needs to happen to turn a negative experience into a positive one is to shift your perspective.

There will always be circumstances and experiences—past and present—that you can't change. But if you'll learn to adjust your interpretation of your experiences, you can rise above the good, bad, and ugly of your past and your current situations. The key is to reframe your view of what you are facing.

Love slows down to reframe your experiences.

What's in a Frame?

A few years ago, I spent a ton of money framing a big picture I love for my office. Just a few weeks after I got it back, I was moving some furniture around and knocked the picture off the wall. The frame bent, and a giant crack formed across the length of the glass. Fortunately, the actual picture wasn't damaged. But I wasn't about to spend more money getting a new frame, so I just hung it up there, broken. Every time I looked at that picture, I wanted to kick myself for being so careless. The cracked frame made the picture look crooked. The most irritating thing about the damage was the fact that anyone who walked into my office felt the need to say, "Hey, there's a crack in that glass." *Thank you, Mr. Observant! Like I didn't know!* It embarrassed me. (There's that link between control-based anger and the fear of embarrassment.) Eventually, I just took the picture off the wall.

Here's the thing. The picture wasn't damaged. The frame just got shattered, and that distorted the picture. All it really needed was a new frame. But the distorted frame was a source of constant irritation for me.

I'm convinced that life is like that picture. Life is what it is. Life is life. It has goods and bads, ups and downs. But what impacts how we see the picture of our life is the frame and glass we put around it.

Fortunately, you can change your frame.

As I already mentioned, the way we see the world tends to be shaped by our past experiences. The past doesn't define you, but it always has an impact on the way we frame up our current situation. Most of our mental blocks come from some sort of wrong interpretation we developed based on a past experience. The people who raised you, where you grew up, how you were treated, the resources you had (or lack of resources you had) all impacted who you are today. Those experiences messed with your frame and are the source of many of your greatest fears. We can't ignore this truth. So to make sure we aren't stuck in fear and anger, we have to slow down and address some of the bad programming—the distorted frames—we have around our past experiences. It's not what happens to you that makes the impact. It's how you interpret what happens to you.

When you want security, connection, or control and instead get abandonment, rejection, humiliation, or any other kind of pain, you develop an explanation (or maybe someone develops it for you) about why the dream didn't happen. We tend to frame it up negatively with a wrong interpretation. *I'm unlovable. I'm not enough. I'm a failure. Everyone is harsh and unloving.* A good sign you have a wrong framework is if you find yourself thinking or saying the words "never" or "always." *I never catch a break. People will always let you down.* Very few things in life are never and always. (Interestingly, God says He will never leave us nor forsake us.[1] And He will always love us. Talk about a great a frame!) If we aren't careful, our whole perspective on life can be tainted by our limited, distorted interpretations of the world—interpretations that aren't even accurate.

A correct interpretation of the truth is where true freedom really starts.

Seeing You for Who You Really Are

A right interpretation of the world starts with seeing yourself correctly. You need to see yourself the way God sees you. Sure, you've made some mistakes. You're probably even doing some self-destructive stuff right now and want to stop. But shame keeps telling you that you aren't worth being loved. You have to understand that no matter what you've done or continue to do, you are still valuable. (If you aren't convinced, I'll prove this when we talk about sacrifice.)

A crumpled and bent one hundred dollar bill hasn't lost a cent of value. And neither have you. You aren't shattered. But the frame you've been seeing yourself through might be. Truth can fix that. This is why what Jesus taught is so powerful. When you accept His gift of salvation, you get reframed. He sees you for what you really are. Paul described the transformation this way: "Therefore, if anyone is in Christ, he is a new creation. The old has passed away; behold, the new has come."[2] Your value comes from Christ in you. There's an amazing promise that comes with that new identity: "And we know that for those who love God all things work together for good, for those who are called according to his purpose."[3] God says it's all gonna work out for good; you just need to adopt His way of seeing things. When you start to get His perspective on your life, you'll be able to release fear and anger. You'll be free to love and be loved. You'll also start to realize that there is a thread of purpose running through the good, bad, and ugly of your story.

Cleaning out the Closet

José grew up in a dysfunctional family full of negativity, jealousy, and downright viciousness. In his teens, he became a victim of cross-border human trafficking. The worst part was that it was his own family who sold him off. Somehow, José managed to keep a good attitude. He worked hard as a slave. But someone lied about him, and he ended up in prison. He refused to get bitter and angry. José ended up helping a fellow prisoner who could have gotten his name cleared, but the guy got out of prison and forgot him. So José continued rotting away in prison.

José had lots of reasons to be angry and resentful—at his family, at his culture, even at God. He got dealt a really bad hand through no fault of his own. He had some physical and emotional scars attached to it all. You can be pretty confident he dealt with major disappointment in those horrible years he spent in slavery and prison.

But then everything changed overnight.

José became the second most powerful man in the country where he had been a slave. José got real, serious power.

Eventually, an economic crisis drove his brothers—the ones who trafficked him—to seek his help. José recognized his brothers, but they didn't recognize him. After using some wise tests to see if they had changed their evil ways, he told them who he was. For obvious reasons, they were terrified. But somewhere along the way, José (by the way, that's his Spanish name—in English, we call him Joseph) had slowed down enough to reframe his circumstances. He had every right to be angry, but instead of being angry and resentful, he said, "As for you, you meant evil against me, but God meant it for good, to bring it about that many people should be kept alive, as they are today."[4]

That is the ultimate example of reframing. It's looking at the big perspective and seeing the good that came from the struggle. Instead of walking around bitter and angry, you recognize that what happens to you isn't the important thing. It's all about the way you choose to look at it. This is not some naive optimism. It's looking at the hard facts. Today, you are something you could not have been otherwise— had it not been for what you went through in the past. Yes, it was horrible. It may still be horrible. But your experience has given you a message to share. If you frame your experience correctly, that message can be a source of love and hope for others.

A person with experience is never at the mercy of someone with a theory. You have experience. Your past pain and hurt give you the authority to speak into the lives of others who are struggling. You can show them just what God can do through someone who refuses to let the true picture of who they are be seen through a distorted or broken frame. You got a new frame. Helps others do the same. That's where you start to find true meaning and purpose. You have a call on your life. Don't get bitter. Get better!

A New Frame

José, a.k.a. Joseph, kept a good attitude and worked hard in the middle of the struggles he faced. He learned about his talent for administration as he ran the entire prison. He learned he had a gift for interpreting dreams. Those skills were ultimately what led to his promotion. I'm convinced, and so was Joseph, that a divine Hand was leading him through all those struggles.

You and I are no different.

God doesn't waste any experience in our lives. What if everything you have faced, or are facing today, is preparation for what's ahead? It's hard to get irritated when you know you're learning something you'll need for the future. (That's why a bunch of the classes I took in school made me angry—I still haven't used them!) If you know you're learning something you'll need, you start paying attention. What if that horrible boss you work for is giving you a paid education in what *not* to do in leadership? What if your struggles with your kids are teaching you more about how God loves you? Don't be afraid or run from your frustrations and challenges—reframe them as training.

Viktor Frankl lived through the horrors of the Holocaust, where millions of his fellow Jews were murdered at the hands of Adolf Hitler. Reflecting, he said, "In some way suffering ceases to be suffering the moment it finds meaning."[5] Your suffering, even the worst kind, can bring meaning if you choose to reframe it. Rather than get angry and bitter, be on the lookout for the good that will surely come from the struggle. Rather than see your life through a frame of fear that those horrible things might happen again, you can be confident that God is at work, no matter how horrible your circumstances are—past or present. You don't have to be afraid of anything when you really believe that God can turn every single thing around for good.

The more you reframe your story, the more it will retrain your brain. You'll get a whole new perspective. Rather than living afraid of having your dreams of security, connection, or control shattered, you'll start to realize that having them shattered doesn't really mean that much in the big picture. It's not the worst thing. Because the reality is that in Christ, even when a dream is shattered, you can be confident that all things will work together for good.

Don't waste your pain and struggle. Don't live in fear that it will always be this way. Don't be anxious and angry. Don't run away. Engage. Reframe it. Get a new perspective. Then you'll be able to trade in a framework of fear for a framework of power, love, and a sound mind. You'll have the authority and strength you need to take responsibility for your life and move ahead with courage and confidence.

8

Take Responsibility

Not everything that is faced can be changed.
But nothing can be changed until it is faced.

—James Baldwin

About a year after we were married, my wife, Emily, and I moved to southern Mexico to run a retreat center. I thought we were going there to teach and minister to locals, but instead, I was about to learn a whole lot. We were right on the Pacific Ocean, and much of my job consisted of fixing anything destroyed by the salty air. Light fixtures, water pumps, air conditioners, you name it—it was constantly rotting. I sprayed things down with fresh water. I coated them with oil. But it just slowed the decay. Something major broke literally every week. I lived in a constant state of frustration and worry, always wondering what was going to break next.

Up to that point in my life, if something broke, I'd just throw my hands up and call a repairman (then get angry about how much they charged) or buy a replacement. I didn't even bother trying to fix things. But my experience in Mexico was about to pull out a side of me I didn't even know was there.

Within three days of arriving, the first challenge came. The freezer we inherited from the previous missionaries broke. I called David, the guy who had lived there before us, and asked him who I should call to fix it.

He laughed. "You have to do it. Nobody will come out there."

So I laughed back. "Bro, I am *not* mechanically inclined."

"Well, you're gonna have to do it. Just take twenty more minutes to really look at it. Look for what seems off."

I didn't want to look at it. I just wanted it fixed. I felt helpless, which quickly led to anger about my circumstances. We were there to minister to people, not fix broken stuff!

After some pouting, I finally surrendered to the fact that I was the one responsible for fixing this. Since I had no idea what I was doing, I called my Mexican friend Max. He came over, grabbed a screwdriver, and just started taking the freezer apart.

I was a bit concerned. "Have you ever done this before?"

He smiled. "No. But we'll figure it out. We just have to look for what looks wrong."

We popped off a few panels and quickly saw it. A "thingy" was cracked and frozen over. We took the "thingy" to a store and said, "*Necesitamos esto.*" ("We need one of these.") We paid a few bucks, took the part home, replaced it, and *voila!* I fixed a freezer (sort of; Max actually did). But I felt back in control of my life.

Over the next six months, I fixed two water pumps, an air conditioner, a hot-water heater, a pool pump, a sewer system, a roof, and several other random things on my own. My control-based anger flared up a lot. Each time I had to remind myself to slow down, fight off feelings of helplessness that were making me angry, and really identify what was causing the problem.

Here's what that experience in Mexico taught me: There are some things in life you can't control—like things breaking down. But there are things you can control—like your attitude and willingness to explore the problem and diagnose it. I learned that, in general, the people who fix things are no smarter than you or me; they just take the time and do the work. In every situation, we have to take the time to figure out what we can control and what we can't. We have to figure out what we're responsible for.

When we face a difficult situation, we usually run to one of two extremes:

- Fight for control and take too much responsibility for something we can't control, which leads to more anger
- Run from the situation because of fear and end up not taking responsibility for something we can actually fix, which can lead to helplessness, victimhood, and anger

In every situation that causes anger and anxiety, we have to slow down and figure out what is and what isn't our responsibility. When we do, it calms our anger and our fear.

Love slows down to evaluate responsibility.

The Responsibility Connection

I spoke to a bunch of pastors recently, and afterward, one of them told me that while I was speaking, he realized he was angry with his congregation and staff. Resentment had been building for years. I offered to meet with him later that afternoon. We talked it through, trying to figure out the *why* of his anger. During the course of the conversation, it became pretty clear that the congregation and staff were actually looking for him to be more assertive.

I asked, "When are you gonna move them forward? They seem frustrated that you aren't leading."

He admitted, "I've been afraid to lead them. They fired the last pastor who made changes in the church." (Unfortunately, I hear this story a lot from pastors.)

I asked how long he had been serving at the church. I was shocked when he said, "Twelve years." It was no wonder frustration was building with him and the congregation. He had put in more than enough time to build the trust he needed to lead, but out of fear of being fired, he wasn't willing to step up and take on his role as leader. He was frustrated and so were the people he was leading.

That's an example of the connection between fear, anger, and taking responsibility. When we're responsible for something and don't step up, it leads to frustration and anger in us and those around us. I know lots of parents who are angry and resentful toward their young children because of how they're behaving. In many of those cases, those angry parents have abdicated their responsibility to slow down and take the time to lovingly discipline their kids. One parent told me, "I'm afraid if I'm too hard on them, they won't love me or they'll rebel." The sad truth is, when we don't take responsibility, someone else will. Someone will influence and raise our kids—culture, TV, the law—and it probably won't be the people we want taking responsibility for them, because they don't truly love them. But you do, which is why getting responsibility right is so important.

People get angry and afraid when those who have responsibility for influence and leadership don't do what they need to do.

David, a fearless shepherd boy, wasn't afraid to face the giant Goliath. But the reason he had to step up was because Saul, the king and commander of the army, was afraid to attack the giant. He had the armor. He had the authority. But he didn't take action. David killed Goliath and led the entire army to victory. He became a hero overnight, and people started singing his praises.

Enter anger.

Saul got angry with David.[1] He set out to kill him. But all David did was step up when no one else would. When people abdicate their responsibilities, it always leads to frustration and anger. Sometimes the anger is in the person who has been living in fear—not taking responsibility for what they need to do. Sometimes the anger is from those who have to carry the responsibility that someone didn't take. I've seen lots of leaders who are burnt-out, bored, or just tired find a new project that excites them—a new business prospect, world missions. They aren't willing to step out and go full-time at the new venture because they need the stability of their income. They end up neglecting their businesses or churches to pursue those new opportunities. Usually the strongest person still at the organization ends up seizing control, either in a power grab or by just trying to survive. But those people who fill in the gap aren't ultimately responsible, so it creates frustration and stress among the staff. The best staff members quit. Lots of people leave angry. All because the leader isn't willing to exert the energy to be responsible for what he has been given. This exact same phenomenon happens when tired parents turn their kids over to TV, teachers, or other adults to raise them. The results are always negative in the long run. That's why it's so important to constantly evaluate our level of responsibility in every situation. When we properly evaluate what we are and aren't responsible for, it brings peace and confidence within us and those we love and lead.

A Swarm of Locus

Figuring out responsibility is tricky. It's a moving target. Something we once had responsibility for may now need to be released. Other times, we take responsibility for things that never were our responsibility. What's truly loving isn't always clearly evident. Sometimes love means going along with people. Other times it means forcing them to take responsibility for their lives.

We have to constantly struggle with the question: *How much of what I'm facing am I responsible for?* You can't take too much responsibility for what is truly your responsibility, but taking responsibility for what isn't your responsibility leads to anger and frustration. Feeling

ongoing anger or resentment about a situation is a good sign that we
haven't properly evaluated our personal responsibility.

In every challenge we face, we land somewhere on a continuum
between taking total responsibility (even if it's not all our responsibility) and taking no responsibility. We tend to make our decisions about
this level of responsibility based on what psychologists call our locus
of control.

Locus of control is how much you believe you control what happens in your life. Locus of control has two extremes: external and
internal.

External Locus of Control————————Internal Locus of Control

It's other people's fault, and I'm helpless to do anything about this.	I'm responsible, my actions make a difference, and I can change things.

Interestingly, the two extremes of mental illness—neuroses and
character disorders—tend to fall on one extreme or the other of that
continuum.

A neurosis is taking total responsibility for everything, even if it's
not your fault. (I tend to be mildly neurotic most of the time.) A character disorder is not taking any responsibility.

The research is pretty clear that people with an internal locus of
control are less likely to be overweight, more likely to describe themselves as healthy, and show lower levels of psychological stress. A
balanced, internal locus of control is the key to living well.

We're complex, so we can have an internal locus of control in one
situation, then later that same day have an external locus of control
in another situation. When life is hard and we're peddling as fast as
we can to keep up, it's easy to lean toward one of the extremes. You
may confidently lead a small army of people at work but feel helpless
against the three-year-old tyrant in your home who refuses to take a

bath. I've met brilliant women and men, people at the top of their fields in business and ministry, who feel helpless to solve problems in their personal lives.

Feeling helpless actually impairs something called executive function. We freeze up and lose our ability to perform tasks we're perfectly capable of performing. Which sounds an awful lot like what happens when we get angry. That's why we have to slow down and really evaluate our level of responsibility when we face challenges; it makes us stronger and wiser.

Here's a sobering truth: most of the time, we have more control than we believe we do—it's just that we're afraid to step up. Responsibility means work. It's a whole lot easier to blame something or someone for our situation. But blaming and feeling like a victim only lead to resentment and anger. Taking responsibility leads to freedom.

Slow Down and Look at It

When something would break on that property in Mexico, I regularly had to remind myself of what my friend David had said. "Just take twenty more minutes to look at it carefully." Really evaluate. Look from multiple angles. If it's a really complex problem, seek outside help. Figure out what you can—and can't—do to resolve this situation.

It's the classic prayer of Reinhold Niebuhr: "God grant me the serenity to accept the things I cannot change, courage to change the things I can, and wisdom to know the difference."

If you think there's really nothing you can do in the face of your current challenges, here's my advice: aim lower. What is the smallest thing you can take responsibility for? There's always something in your power to change. It may be as simple as your attitude. You may need to reframe what's happening. You may never be able to change your boss or your spouse, but you can change your attitude. And you are the only one who can change your attitude. It may seem tiny or insignificant in the face of an even bigger problem, but don't worry about the bigger problem—do what you can do. It's pretty common that when you take responsibility for what you can change—stop ignoring bad behavior, stop checking out, lovingly and wisely discipline the kids—other things start to change.

Take an honest look at your life right now. What are you responsible for that, with a little work, you could actually change right now? There's a good chance there's something you can change that you've been afraid to take responsibility for. Afraid of the work involved. Afraid you might fail. If you've been running from responsibility, please, please, please go face it! Have the conversation. Fill out the paperwork. Look at the debt balance. Just face it. Don't back down. Blaming is easy, but blaming leads to victimhood and anger. You can't fix everything, but you can fix some things. You are far more capable than you give yourself credit for. God can give you the strength to do what you need to do. The best news is that if you'll do your part, God will come in and do what you can't do on your own. Remember, "God gave us a spirit not of fear but of power and love and self-control."[2] Taking control of yourself gives you power to make the small changes that lead to big changes. Start small. Do what you can do right now.

Living in fear always drives us to go faster and do more and more. It leads to imbalance. It causes stress and anxiety. It's exhausting. But when we have the courage to take proper responsibility, we won't be consumed with fear and anger. You'll do what you can do and let go of what you can't do anything about. Once you've got a picture of what you can and can't control, you'll begin seeing a lot more clearly. And that's when you can figure out if all the running and building and acquiring is really getting you what you want. There's a good chance fear-based living has filled your plate with more than you can handle. And you are tired. You don't need to do more. What you need is to create space for what is truly most important. And that's what we'll look at next.

PART III

Create Space

9

Choose What to Lose

A traveler is happier the lighter his load.

—*Marcus Felix*

Most of the people who go on expeditions with me have never done a major hike before. Which is what I want. I'm not looking for people who are all wildernessy and willing to chop off their arm with a Swiss Army knife to survive. Those people would be really out of place on my teams. (Plus, I don't want them around—they'll make me look like a wimp!)

Because the people in my groups are all first-timers, they're usually really concerned about having the correct gear. I get tons of texts and emails asking exactly what they should bring. So before our trips, I give them a packing list and have them watch a video I recorded about how to pack for a hike. I show them exactly what I bring. I want them to feel confident without over-packing, but most team members still bring way too much with them. (Some commission-based salesperson at the outdoor store probably saw them coming and convinced them they needed every gadget possible or they would die on a mountain.) They show up for the hike loaded down with gear.

This is a serious problem.

A pack that's too heavy will wear you out, and you won't be able to successfully complete the hike. So the night before we leave for the trail, I'll often do a gear weigh-in. I set a weight goal for their bags. If it's too heavy, I have them start pulling stuff out of it.

This process gets highly emotional in a hurry. People get really sensitive about their stuff. I've seen grown men—CEOs of large organizations—nearly in tears when I have them leave some things behind. Some folks even get angry. One girl who I wouldn't let bring a hairdryer (on a trail that had no electricity!) was mad at me for days. As I lighten their loads, I can see the fear in their eyes—but I know they'll get over it. Usually by the second day of the hike, those same people thank me for making them lighten their loads. They realize just how hard the hike would have been with all that extra weight.

I'm convinced that nobody intends to overpack. It happens slowly, little by little. We're afraid of not having something we may need, so we just take everything. It's wise to prepare, but you can't prepare for everything. We end up overloaded and tired. By the way, I'm not talking about packing for a trip anymore. I'm talking about life.

Life is like a long hike, and most of us are walking along with a pack that is way too heavy. We're all doing our best to provide for our families and give them the opportunities we never had. We figure if we can just get a little more, we'll have everything we need. But slowly, little by little, we get overloaded.

Our finances are overloaded. We spend everything we make, or more.

Our time is overloaded. Work deadlines, overtime, kids' sports schedules.

Our energy is overloaded. I heard someone say, "The world is run by tired people." Basically, yes.

Like a hiker picking up rocks along the trail, thinking we might need them at some point to throw at a bear or lion, we take on more and more. A lot of what we add to our load is actually good stuff—opportunities, relationships. But as the weight builds, we feel overwhelmed, like we're carrying around a giant pack. We're strong. But not that strong. We end up tired and dread every day, saying, "Again? I'm tired and I can't carry all this anymore."

At some point, we have to slow down (maybe even stop) and really look at what we're bringing with us. We have to figure out if all the stuff we're carrying is helping us or hindering us in getting to where we want to be. At some point, we have to decide to leave a few things behind.

Love slows down to choose what to lose.

Define the Destination

We all have an idea in mind of what the good life looks like. We have a destination in mind. Sometimes we get those ideas from how we were raised. Other times we get them from other people telling us what we should want—what makes for the good life. We may never write it down or say it out loud, but we all have a picture of what having security, connection, and control looks like—a nice home, a loving marriage, kids who go further than we ever did in education or work. It's good to have a goal. You need something to aim at. King Solomon said, "Where there is no prophetic vision the people cast off restraint...."[1] A prophetic vision is just a mental picture of where you want to go. If you don't know where you're going, it's really easy to "cast off restraint" and just take everything—even things you don't really need.

When you know where you want to go, you'll know what to pack. And what not to pack. You don't pack flip-flops to climb through the snows of Mount Kilimanjaro. You don't take a warm goose-down parka for hiking through the Amazon. Life is no different. When you know where you want to go, it's a lot easier to know what to bring with you and what needs to be left behind.

When we've decided where we want to go in life, we start packing accordingly. We fill our lives with whatever promises to get us the security, connection, or control we want for our families and ourselves. Anything that you believe will get you where you want to go has value to you. But if we aren't careful, we can add so much to our lives that we actually start to weigh ourselves down. Rather than improve our chances of getting us to our destinations, without realizing it, we can actually hinder our abilities in the long run. So to do a good gear check for your life, you need to start by looking at what you value.

A Question of Values

I hear this line a lot: "I really want to travel more, but it's so expensive. How can you afford to travel so much?" They look at my beat-up fifteen-year-old car, and it's pretty clear that I'm not rolling in money. And they are correct. But that old car is a big part of the reason I can afford to travel so much.

Having a nice, new car isn't that important to me. But travel is. So rather than making a car payment every month, I take what would have been spent on the payment and divide it up into savings—a little for travel and a little for when we'll need a new (older) car. Emily and I both value travel, so we decided to live in a house that is worth way less than what we can afford. When we travel, we do it cheaply. We travel with friends and split costs. In fact, we can do a two-week trip to Europe for what most people spend on four months of car payments. We value travel more than having a new car, so we do whatever it takes to scrimp and save to do it. There is absolutely nothing wrong with having a nice, dependable vehicle. (Honestly, sometimes we do get a little jealous of people with nice, shiny cars with no dents in them.) There's nothing wrong with having a big, beautiful, expensive home. It's just that travel is more important to us than those things. So we put our money, time, and energy toward travel.

We all have certain things that we value—travel, a nice home, a secure job, loving relationships, respect. Values are unique to each person, and there are an unlimited number of things you can value. Some of our values are learned through how we were raised. Some are just adopted—without much question—based on the society or culture we live in. And the truth is, many of our values come from doing whatever it takes to make sure the thing we fear the most doesn't come upon us. We may not be sure exactly what we want, but we know what we *don't* want. And we run as fast as we can away from those things. When we live in fear, we tend to value whatever will remove the fear that threatens us.

We naturally give our time, money, and energy to those things that we believe will get us where we want to go or keep us away from what we fear the most. That's part of what Jesus was talking about when He said, "Where your treasure is, there will your heart be also."[2] If you want to know what your heart is set on, look at where you spend your time, money, and energy (your treasures). In other words: Our actions always show what we truly value. If you want to know what you really value, look at what you do—not what you say or think or feel.

If you work a lot of hours, then work and financial security are probably values for you.

If you engage in all sorts of online debates and always want the latest gossip, then drama has a high value for you.

If you exercise a lot, health or how you look is of high value.

What we do makes it clear what we really value. We naturally give our time, money, and energy to what we truly value most.

I drive an old car. Now I would love to travel and also be able to drive a new car, but my bank account tells me that's just not possible. I've only got so much income and so much money. And this is the challenge we all eventually face.

We are limited.

We only have so much time, money, and energy. Because we're limited, we're forced to figure out what is truly of highest value at some point. Not every value can have equal value. If everything has the same value, nothing has value. You can be certain that if you are trying to give everything equal value, you'll experience lots of anger and anxiety. You'll also get really tired.

There needs to be a hierarchy to our values. Some things have to be more important than others. And sometimes things that are of lesser importance will have to be pulled out of our pack and left behind. Sometimes we have to sacrifice good things to give our best to the best things.

The Right Sacrifice

The first time we read about anger in the Bible is also the first time we read about sacrifice. Cain and his brother Abel bring an offering—a sacrifice—to God. For some reason, God rejects Cain's offering.

Cain gets angry.

God asks him, "Why are you angry, and why has your face fallen? If you do well, will you not be accepted? And if you do not do well, sin is crouching at the door. Its desire is contrary to you, but you must rule over it."[3]

The word translated "sin" (*chata*) in this verse comes from an archery term that means "to miss the mark." God basically tells Cain that he aimed wrong. He missed it. He had the wrong goal. God didn't value what Cain valued, so his sacrifice didn't count.

There are wrong sacrifices.

I talk to people all the time who realized too late that they sacrificed their marriage for their career. Hospitals are filled with people who sacrificed their health for the sake of pleasure and convenience. Lots of people sacrifice their long-term relationship with their kids, all in the name of providing financial security for them. They spend hours away from their families to provide them with money, but what the family really wants is their presence.

Here's the really hard pill to swallow: You can live a morally upright life—be faithful to your wife, pay your taxes, provide for your family. But if you value the wrong things, you can end up feeling the same negative results as actual sin—remorse and regret.

A pastor recently shared with me that he was angry and resented his wife for leaving him. He humbly bragged about how he had been faithful to her, prayed for her, and loved her. He made lots of sacrifices to be in the ministry. He was angry at his spouse and kids for not being supportive of the "call" on his life. But his wife was angry too. She said he put ministry to others ahead of caring for his own family. After some soul-searching, he admitted that he had sacrificed his family for the affirmation he got from always being available to his church. He made a lot of sacrifices for ministry, but he sacrificed the wrong things.

It's possible to be very sincere and loyal to those you love but still make the wrong sacrifice. You can aim wrong. You have to keep a constant eye on what is really being sacrificed. What makes this even more challenging is the fact that values are a moving target. In the next chapter, we'll see that some values shouldn't change, but lots of them have to be adjusted based on what season of life you're in. When seasons change—you get married, have kids, change jobs, make transitions, kids leave the house—you will need to make some changes to your value structure. If you are still doggedly pursuing goals that you set for yourself in your teens, twenties, or thirties without making adjustments for new values that have appeared since then—like kids and a spouse—there's a good chance some of your values that arrived more recently on the scene may be suffering because of it. Some values should change with new seasons.

So how do you know if a value needs to change? Great question. Fortunately, there's a pretty simple sign that your values may need to be adjusted. You just have to go back and visit with your friendly personal consultant. Anger or frustration in yourself or those around you is a good sign that some values might need adjustment. It's a sign that you may need to change some priorities to make sure you're only carrying what you need for this phase of your journey.

Get honest about where you are in life. Is there an issue that is constantly a point of contention in your home or work? Is there something that is always igniting anger in you or those around you? Is it possible that something you truly value is unintentionally getting less time, energy, or money than it deserves? What do your actions show that you really value? I'd encourage you to take some time to compare what you say you value and what your actions say you value. If you've never thought through what you really value, consider writing it out. Often just taking the time to slow down and define what you really value—writing it down—can help relieve the tension.

After looking at your life and evaluating what you're carrying, you may decide you need to leave a few things behind. Letting some things go isn't failure. It's actually success. It may be hard, but I'm pretty sure you won't regret lightening your load. A traveler is happier the lighter his or her load is. Which is why it's so important to get really clear about where you want to go and what you value. Something always has to be sacrificed to make room for what's most important. Knowing exactly what to sacrifice means you need to prioritize.

10

Prioritize

Perfection is attained not when there is
nothing more to add,
but when there is nothing more to remove.

—Antoine de Saint-Exupéry

Shortly after we were married, Emily and I moved to Cusco, Peru, to help some folks start a church and café. We had only been married for two years, but we had accumulated quite a bit of stuff, thanks to wedding gifts and setting up our own house. I really liked all the things we had picked out, but when I saw how much it would cost to ship it all to Peru, I decided it would be cheaper to just sell our big items and buy everything there. We only took two bags each, and because of airline restrictions (and my being cheap), those bags had to be under fifty pounds.

Trying to figure out the bare minimum to start a new life in another country was pretty stressful. Even more challenging was the fact that we didn't know exactly what we were getting into—we had never actually been to Cusco. So I had to guess at what I'd need. I settled on my guitar, my computer, and clothes. Everything else stayed behind. A few months after we moved, people started bringing us some of the items we didn't bring. Funny thing was, by then I had forgotten about a lot of that stuff. I lived a rich, full life without it for months.

A few years later, we moved back to the United States and had to do the process all over again. Some things that I had taken down were left in Peru so I'd have room to bring back things that were now more important to me.

King Solomon said there's a time and season for everything in life.[1] What's important in one season may not be quite as important in another. Nothing stays the same in life—including what we value. What is really important in one season may become completely irrelevant in another. Life is constantly changing, and if we don't adapt, it will just lead to anger and frustration. We have to prioritize what is truly most important in every season.

Love slows down to prioritize.

A Moving Target

When my daughter was first born, I started getting angry a lot. I wasn't hitting things or yelling at people. It was the kind of anger that's sitting just below the surface, ready to erupt—sometimes at the smallest frustrations. I didn't take it out on people; I'd just get furious at myself for not getting enough done. I felt stuck. I was no fun to be around.

It took me about three years, but I finally realized that having a kid changes everything. *Ev*-e-ry-thing. (Yes, it took three years. I'm slow.) Life had completely changed, but I was still trying to live the same way I always had. Emily and I used to travel all over the place on a whim. (She's a flight attendant, so it was easy to just pick a flight that had open seats and take off. We always had tons of flexibility.) Also, I prided myself on how efficient I was. I used to be able to get a bunch of stuff done in one day. I also used to be able to sleep. All that changed the day my daughter was born.

Now, I said I understood that life changes when you have kids, but I thought I was pretty invincible, so I hadn't actually changed anything in my life. I just added a new value to the bag. I was still mentally trying to live by an old value system—which was great for that season. It was all good stuff. But seasons had changed. A new value—a big one, my daughter—came in and took the place of traveling, productivity, flexibility, and sleep. Using my time, energy, and money in the same way as before my daughter was born left me tired and frustrated.

Anger and frustration don't just happen with kids. They come with any transition or season change. A new job. Kids getting older and leaving the house. A relationship ending. Getting married. Moving to a new place. Losing a loved one. When life changes, new things will need to be embraced and other things will need to be left behind; otherwise you'll start to feel frustration with yourself and with those around you.

After some soul-searching, I decided I needed to write down what's most important in this season of life. Here's the values hierarchy I developed for myself:

Relationship with God
Being present for my wife
Being present for my daughter
Caring for my health
Providing financially
Work/ministry

Because I'm always running so hard toward my goals, I don't usually realize a value is out of order until I start feeling tension between me and my wife. She'll get frustrated that I'm spending too much time at work. (Which is really complicated because I work from home!) I feel like I manage the work-life balance well, but on a regular basis right before dinner, I'll run upstairs to get something from my office and notice an email came in that I need to respond to. Rather than wait, I'll respond. Twenty minutes later, I'm still working. And my wife is irritated. Do this for a few days in a row and a real problem arises. Whenever my lesser value (work) gets more time, money, or energy than a higher value (my wife and daughter), it's not long before someone gets frustrated.

I've heard so many stories of similar conflicts of values when seasons change.

A lady who had been a single mother for twelve years told me she had recently gotten married. For the last twelve years, her son and her job had been two of her highest values. But now her new husband entered into her value system. She was only a few months into the marriage, but she was getting into lots of fights with her new husband. Most of the fights revolved around him feeling like he was coming in second place to her son. She had some pretty solid logic for why: "I know God says my husband needs to be first. But he may leave me, like the last guy did. And my son will always be my son." Deep down she was afraid, understandably, that her new husband might leave and that her son would be resentful of losing his place in the hierarchy. Then she'd lose everything she valued.

A new value (her husband) had appeared, but she was struggling to make the adjustment to the new value system. Understandably, it was scary to rearrange her values. Making the right sacrifice can be a true test of faith.

I've also talked to newlyweds who complain that their spouse is still living like a single person—hanging out with friends away from their spouse until late in the night. It creates anger and resentment because one partner didn't change his or her value system when they got married.

If you have kids, you know they require tons of sacrifice. Caring for them can become all-consuming. We have to make sure that we don't sacrifice our spouse to our kids. The kids will leave the house one day, but you'll want your spouse around until death do you part.

We only have our kids for a short time, which is why sometimes those resume-building, extracurricular activities they are part of need to be sacrificed: they've slipped in and eroded your value of family time and home or church. I can't tell you how many parents I meet who are angry and resentful of their kids' sports schedules and ballet classes. They feel like they're driving all over creation all the time. There's nothing wrong with activities, but when they intrude on higher values, you can be sure it will cause some anger and irritation—and probably some exhaustion.

There will be times that we have to let go of good, fun things because they're just causing too much strain. We may not get as much accomplished, or as quickly as we'd like. But if it's because you are living by higher values, you can lay your head to rest at night with a sense of peace—you lived by your values. No, the porch didn't get painted this weekend, but you finally got to spend some quality time with your increasingly elusive teenage daughter—and she'll be out of the house sooner than you know it. You can paint the porch then! You didn't get the extra money for working on the weekend, but you went to the men's event at your church and realized some things you can do to improve your marriage.

We don't have to be angry because something didn't get done. Something DID get done. We lived out our values.

Taking Aim

If something in your life is causing ongoing anger and frustration, don't just tolerate it. Evaluate it. Do a priority check. But to properly evaluate it, you'll need to do two specific things:

1. Figure out what you really value.
2. Make a list. Put it in numerical order. Put what is most important at top, then go from there. Get honest about it. Look at what you do—that always reveals what you

really value. Then see if it lines up with what you say or think you value.

3. Identify the tension point (that is, consult your anger).
4. Ask yourself where there's tension in your hierarchy of values. What are fights and frustrations with those you love always about? Is the tension point something on the list of what you value most? Is that issue not even on the list? Where do you feel unfulfilled or frustrated? Is it possible that a lesser value is getting higher priority than it should?

There are an unlimited number of things you can value. And values change. But there are some values you'll need in your pack, no matter where the journey of life may take you. And you can be certain that if you keep those values close, you will find love, joy, and peace in your life. So what are those non-negotiables? Well, for that we simply need to get input from a Guide who knows the trail better than anyone.

Getting the Order Right

Jesus understood the challenge of being human. He understood the fear and anxiety—and even the anger—of what it's like living in this world. He said: I know you're worried and anxious about what you'll eat, where you'll live, and all the other concerns around having security, connection, and control, "but seek first the kingdom of God and his righteousness, and all these things will be added to you."[2]

God created you. He knows what you need. But Jesus says the way you get what you need is counterintuitive. If you want security, connection, and control, don't focus on them; focus on what God values first. Make His values your values, and you'll get it all. You will only be fulfilled and at peace when you value what He values.

So what does God value most?

Well, Jesus kept the packing list pretty simple. When a wealthy young man approached him and asked for the bottom line—what was most important in life—Jesus narrowed it down to this: Love God and love people.[3] That's it.

1. God
2. People

Wanting God's way above our way should always be first. If God clearly said, "Don't do this," then don't bring it with you. Don't put it in your pack. It'll wear you out. Valuing what God values is the top priority. And right after God, the second most important thing you can value is relationships with people.

If you really want your priorities in line, you can be certain that relationships with people are always of higher value than money, work, success, security, or control. Some relationships need to be more important than others. If you are married, your spouse should always be way up there on the values. In fact, I'm convinced that our spouse should be in the spot just below God.

Let me explain.

The Greatest Sacrifice

Something always has to be sacrificed for what is of highest value. So God set the example.

God loved the world (people) so much that He gave (sacrificed) His only Son, so whoever believes in Him would not perish, but have everlasting life.[4]

You and I are of so much value that God sacrificed His Son. When I think back to the order of my top three highest values—God, my wife, and my daughter—I realize that God set that order first. God's people, the Church, are called the Bride of Christ. God was willing to sacrifice His own Son for our sake.

But that's wasn't the end. God sacrificed His Son, but then the very thing He sacrificed was brought back to life. Sometimes we'll sacrifice something for a greater value in one season, and God will bring it back to life in a resurrected, more glorious form. You may sacrifice a dream to raise a family, and find that God resurrects that dream later in life. It's never too late. One touch of God's favor can change everything. He can bring it back to life. But it starts when you value what He values—in the order He values it—then choose to let go of things that are of lesser value.

The Apostle Paul talks about how Abel's sacrifice still speaks today because it was the right sacrifice.[5] Our decision to make the right sacrifices is about more than just us. The right sacrifices can outlive us. They can live on in our kids and in the organizations we lead. But we have to be willing to lay them aside first before we get the better versions. The right sacrifices can have a world-changing impact.

Making Space for the Best

You can't carry it all. You only have so much time, money, and energy. What will you leave behind today? What are you going to take out of your pack that snuck in there? What are you going to stop doing? What are you going to let go of? It may be scary. You may have to lay down some values you've held on to since your teens or twenties. The sacrifice may seem too much. But I'm convinced you can't sacrifice for God. He won't let you. The minute you think you've given something up, He'll open the windows of Heaven and pour out blessings you never could have imagined. It won't be a sacrifice. You'll find it was really just creating space for greater things He had for you.

11

Create Space

God is always trying to give good things to us,
but our hands are too full to receive them.

—*Saint Augustine*

While I was in college, I went to visit a missionary friend of mine who lived in Latin America. The first evening I was there, I asked him, "What exactly do you do all day?"

He said, "I'll show you tomorrow."

We got up early and pulled out some tools for a construction project. But just as we started cutting wood, someone showed up and asked if we could help do some electrical wiring at a widow's house. We hopped in the truck and spent most of the morning working on the project.

After lunch, we got started cutting wood again, but another guy arrived and asked if we could pray for a family member who was dying. We went over and prayed for the guy, then spent a few minutes consoling the family.

We got back and started to work on the construction again, but a young adult came by and wanted some advice on something or other. At this point, I was starting to get really frustrated. *How does he get anything done around here?* The rest of the day was filled with little distractions. That night, I commented about how little had gotten done today and said, "Maybe tomorrow you can show me what you do."

He laughed. "Dude, you already saw it. That's what I do. My ministry is distractions. I leave room for those distractions God sends my way."

I'll never forget that response. It was the total opposite of how I was living at the time. I had no room for anything extra. I knew where I needed to be every minute of the day. Full-time work, full-time college, I played in a band, and I even had a girlfriend for a while. It was all good stuff. I enjoyed what I was doing. But I felt completely overwhelmed, and I thought that's how life was supposed to be—packed with busyness.

I know you can relate. Our time is maxed out. Between work, school schedules, sports practice, weekend tournaments, church events, and just the general responsibilities of life, we're constantly busy. Our finances are maxed out. There are mortgages, rent, and college loans. There's no room for error. One problem—a flat tire, an emergency room visit—throws everything into chaos. When we have nothing to give, it causes anxiety, depression, anger, or makes us just want to give up on life. As we discussed in the last chapter, something has to give at some point. Something has to be sacrificed for what's most important. When we sacrifice, we create space, and that space leaves room for all sorts of amazing possibilities.

Love slows down to create space.

It's Getting Brighter in Here

When I was a kid, I remember entering the home of a distant aunt of mine after she passed away. She was a hoarder. Every nook and cranny of the house was packed with stuff. Stuff that I'm sure she was certain she might need. Stuff was piled so high that all the windows were blocked, and light couldn't even get in. Constantly adding more to our lives can lead to some pretty dark places.

I love Proverbs 4:18: "The path of the righteous is like the light of dawn, which shines brighter and brighter until full day." It's a promise that the best is yet to come, no matter how dark and dreary things may seem now. Here's the thing: The path of the righteous is bright, but too often, we have packed every space in our lives with what we believe will give us security, connection, and control. The stuff piled around the windows of our souls has blocked out the light of dawn. In the words of Saint Augustine, "God is always trying to give good things to us, but our hands are too full to receive them."

It's like when you go on vacation with a full suitcase, then find that perfect souvenir—but have no space to bring it back with you. You have to choose between either not getting the cool souvenir, leaving something behind, or buying a bigger bag. And if you do get another bag, you'll probably have to pay some crazy-expensive luggage fees to the airline! If we aren't careful, our lives can become a full suitcase with no room left for anything better that God might have for us.

I regularly work with people in my coaching program who want a more fulfilling job, but they can't afford to take one that pays less because their mortgage is based on their current level of income. They are blessed with a nice, expensive house, but it means they have to keep working to pay for it. When there's no margin, there's no room for any new adventure or opportunity that might come along.

Whether it's our income, our time, or our energy, we naturally tend to fill in any empty spaces in our lives. Sometimes we fill gaps out of fear. Sometimes it's because we feel a need to prove ourselves and want to justify our existence on the planet by staying busy. Sometimes it's just because we want to soak up every last drop of life. But when there's no margin, we can actually end up missing out on opportunities. Someone may offer last-minute tickets to a professional sports event or concert, but we can't take them because every night of the week is completely booked. Living this way leads to feeling trapped—trapped in our jobs, trapped in our houses, trapped in debt. Being trapped is a horrible feeling (especially for someone with control-based anger!).

Fortunately, there's another way.

One of the most faith-filled decisions we can make is to intentionally create space in our lives. Choosing not to overload our finances, time, and energy is essentially a step of faith, saying, "I know there's so much good out there that I'm gonna leave space for it when it gets here."

God wants to do amazing things in our lives. But He isn't going to force His way in. We have to make the space for Him.

Strategic Space

For several years, I led four-month backpacking trips through Asia and Central America. Most of the team thought I had the whole trip planned out. But I didn't. I nailed down the round-trip flights and the first week or two of the adventure. But that was it. Some of the more Type-A team members were always asking me to give them the "plan." I told them it was on a need-to-know basis, but I didn't actually know the entire plan. I'm a Type-A person, but I learned early on that it's important to leave open space in our schedule. Mainly because traveling, especially in the developing world, requires tons of flexibility. But also, some of the most memorable experiences—sleeping in yurts on the Mongolian steppe, exploring recently discovered ancient ruins in the jungles of Central America—never would have happened if I hadn't left space.

Not filling every moment also meant there were days when we didn't have anything to do. But I don't regret those days. In fact, some of the best talks I had with team members—life-changing, course-altering talks—came on those days. On one stretch of down days, a girl on our team realized she wasn't supposed to marry the guy she was engaged to. She broke it off! Doing "nothing" gave her time to really figure out what she wanted. Sometimes doing nothing is the most valuable thing you can do.

When was the last time you had nothing to do? Literally nothing?

I think it's really hard for some of us to slow down and take a day for nothing because we feel like we're being irresponsible. There's always more we could do. Some people worry that they'll get left behind if they do nothing. We tend to pride ourselves on how busy we are, as if that means we're accomplishing something valuable. I heard Bob Goff say once, "It's easy to confuse a lot of activity with a purposeful life." I tend to believe that staying busy justifies my existence. I can even convince myself that what I'm doing is for God—it's God's work. But honestly, a lot of what I fill my time with is just my attempt to keep from feeling worthless or out of control of my life.

I know that some reading this will look around and think, *It's just not possible to create more space or align where I am with the values I really want.* I get it. Sometimes other people's decisions, betrayal, bureaucracy, and just plain obnoxiousness can put you in positions where it feels like survival mode is the only option. I completely understand. There will be some seasons of challenge, some circumstances where you just can't create more space in your time, money, or energy. But don't give up hope. Rather than become resentful or depressed, in that moment, ask yourself what small step you can take to get closer to the target. Aim low. It may be as small as being grateful for something in your life. Once you've taken that small step, look up and reevaluate. What's the next small step you can take? Sooner or later, if you keep taking small steps toward the target, you'll get close enough to hit it—and you'll be able to create more space in your life.

Space for Connection

When my daughter comes home from school, the first thing I ask her is "How was school?" She gives me facts. What she learned, what she did. Which is nice to know, but I usually want to know how she was treated and the interactions she had with others. Those don't come out on demand. Sometimes we'll be sitting at a stoplight and—out of the blue—she'll tell me another kid was mean to her days earlier. She had to process it for a while before it came out. If I hadn't left space (in this case, by keeping the radio off in the car), there's a good chance I wouldn't have gotten the information I really wanted.

I learned early on in counseling that the most important parts of the conversation don't happen until after the person explains the "facts" of what's happening around them. Before most of us can explain what is happening *in* us, we have to first express what is happening *to* us. Once the "facts" are out of the way, we start to address our interpretations and feelings about those facts. That's how we get to the heart of our feelings of frustration, discouragement, and anger. But it takes time and space for those true feelings to emerge.

Getting to the important stuff in a relationship takes time. Time is our most valuable asset. You can always get more money. But they aren't making more time. If you really love someone, the most important thing you can give them is time and space in conversation.

If you are married or ever plan to be, you need to make time and space for conversation a priority. It is really, really, really important. Real, true conversation requires a lot of space. Tension has been building between you and your partner, but neither of you knows why. You just know you aren't happy. Most of us need to talk it out to realize what we're really feeling.

I'm the world's worst at planning dates. They just seem like lots of energy and money that we don't need to spend. But planning a date night is a powerful statement. It's a statement of value to your spouse. When you carve out time, money, and energy to just focus on your spouse, it shows you value them. Creating space for focused time with people you love should be a priority if you want healthy relationships.

Creative Space

Teresa Amabile, a Harvard researcher, found that people under high levels of time pressure are 45 percent less likely to come up with creative solutions because they're constantly operating under something she calls "pressure hangover."[1] Scott Barry Kaufman did a bunch of surveys and found that 72 percent of people have their best ideas in the shower.[2] Know why? They were relaxed and not under pressure.

I think that's why God asks us to take a mandatory break once per week. He asks us to stop working, stop trying to provide, and just chill out and leave some space. We need time to let Him restore us. We'll talk more about rest in a few chapters, but know this: your creativity depends on leaving space. When you are constantly under pressure, you cannot come up with your best, most creative solutions.

Your best ideas, strongest relationships, and greatest adventures will come when you create space. What could your life look like if you had a little more space in your time, money, and energy? From personal experience, I'll tell you it eliminates a lot of frustration and anxiety. Imagine having a few nights a week where you just chill at home. Imagine having some extra money at the end of the month because you chose to downsize a little. Can you imagine the level you could operate at if you had more energy? I'm convinced we aren't supposed to live burned out and exhausted. But if we aren't intentional, life will crowd every empty space in our lives. When we choose to make some sacrifices and prioritize to make space, it will bring peace.

Get serious about giving yourself some breathing room. Drop an activity or two. Buy a house or car that is less than what you can afford so you'll have money to be generous or travel. Schedule fewer meetings, but give the people you do meet with lots more time. Get creative on how you will make some space.

But the most important thing to remember is this: Once you have the space—don't fill it back in! Leave the space.

12

Course-Correct

*Discipline means to prevent everything in your life
from being filled up.
Discipline means that somewhere you're not occupied,
and certainly not preoccupied.
In the spiritual life, discipline means to create that space in
which something can happen that you hadn't planned or
counted on.*

—Henri Nouwen

One of my all-time favorite Summit Leaders adventures was a sailing trip to Dry Tortugas National Park off the coast of Florida. A friend met us in Key West with his Amel Super Maramu sailboat. He gave us a quick lesson on sailing, and we headed out into open ocean.

Throughout the journey, we all took turns at the helm driving the ship. Someone always had to be on watch for what was ahead. On the dashboard near the helm, there was a small digital GPS map with our destination and information about our heading. You'd think we could've just pointed the boat in the right direction and then walked away for a while. But we couldn't. Sailing required constant course correction because the boat was always being pushed off our straightest route by ocean currents and wind. If we just left the boat alone, it would naturally veer off course.

Just like driving that boat, living life well requires constant course correction. You have to stay vigilant and alert to make sure you're heading toward your most important values. There will always be outside forces that subtly push us away from what we value most.

Most of us can spot major changes quickly. They are like a big gust of wind that blows the boat off course. We immediately notice what happened. But what tends to sneak up on us are the parts of life that accumulate slowly. The currents and gentle breezes. Possessions. Responsibilities. We add a little here and a little there. Life gets a little more hectic. But it's subtle. We end up like a frog in a pot of water. The water warms so slowly that we don't realize it until we're boiling with anger or trembling with anxiety.

When the pressure has built, the answer is never to go faster. You have to slow down and make sure you're heading where you want to be. You will never make up with speed what you lack in direction.

Love slows down to course-correct.

Stop Doing That

For many years, I started my Inca Trail hike with a one-day white-water rafting trip. The goal was to acclimatize to the eleven-thousand-foot altitude in Cusco, where the team met for the hike. That rafting day was stressful. We'd always return late and be crunched for time as we did the final packing and weighing of our gear. I'd get angry at the outfitters if they were too slow while packing up the rafts or getting us back to the hotel. I was grumpy and didn't look forward to the start of the trip because I hated the stress it caused me. This happened year after year.

One day on the ride back from that rafting trip, right in the middle of my anger and frustration, I had an epiphany. *This isn't working.* For some reason, I thought we *had* to go rafting to acclimatize. But the fact is, the Inca Trail starts at a much lower altitude than Cusco (seven thousand feet). It hit me. *We don't have to go rafting. The team will be fine.*

So I stopped doing it.

It created instant relief. It also allowed me to lower the cost of my trip, and we started the hike sooner. I don't know why it took me so long to figure it out. I had some sort of mental block. I had toilet paper rolls over my eyes. I thought things had to be a certain way, but they didn't. When I finally slowed down to think it through, I realized I could stop.

It's easy to get stuck in patterns that once served a purpose. But now we may just be doing it out of habit. In his book *The Power of Habit*, Charles Duhigg explains that well over half of what we do is habit-based.[1] Our brain can only process so much information, so it uses patterns and habits to save brain power. But our tendency to develop habits means we're prone to make the same mistakes over and over—even if they're causing frustration or anger. We'll do what's familiar most of the time. It may be dysfunctional, but at least we know what to expect. If we don't recognize that a pattern is causing problems, we rarely abandon it. Instead, we just dive back into a dysfunctional pattern. We keep driving the boat ahead, slowly veering further and further off course. We think, *It'll be different this time.* But unless we've evaluated the patterns and decisions we made, it probably won't be.

I work with lots of folks who have been recently divorced. Divorce can feel like a full-frontal assault on security, connection, and control. For obvious reasons, people do what they can to get away from feeling threatened in those areas. I meet lots of people who jump right into another relationship after a divorce. Getting back in a relationship promises to calm the pain and meet their needs of security, connection, and control. Sadly, lots of people end up right back in another unhealthy relationship—just like what caused their first marriage to end. It's familiar. But it leads to the same results. They say that the definition of insanity is doing the same thing over and over and expecting different results. At some point, you have to slow down to recognize the patterns in your life—the ways you tend to look for security, connection, or control that are unhealthy—and then make corrections to really get healthier and stronger.

Stopping Isn't Failure

When you decide to give something your time, energy, or money, you need to ask if it truly serves your values. If it's not serving your overall aim, you need to at least consider stopping.

Stopping isn't failure. Some things need to end. If your value system is constantly making you anxious, angry, and stressed, you really should slow down to evaluate what's happening. Don't just tolerate dysfunction. If it's something you can stop—then stop! There's no shame in stopping. In fact, it actually shows you are mentally healthy.

Sometimes this means drastic changes. You may need to start looking for another job. You may need to drive a cheaper car or live in a smaller house because the stress is just getting to be too much. But more often than not for most of us, it just requires a few tweaks. We need to say no to a few good things to make room for the best things. The key is to constantly evaluate if your time, money, and energy are truly going toward what is most important.

Try this. Make a list of what takes up most of your resources.

Take an honest look at your time. What do you spend your waking hours doing? Driving? Paperwork? Cooking?

Make a list of where your money goes. (Yes, this is called a budget, but I know better than to use that word!) Is your money going toward the things that serve your goals in life?

What takes up most of your physical energy? Does it take energy away from what you really want to give it to?

Figure out where all your resources are going. Then ask yourself, "Is this accomplishing what I really want?"

Here's an exercise I do with folks in my coaching program that helps bring lots of clarity:

Draw two circles.

Make the first circle into a pie chart of what is taking most of your time or money or energy. You can use percentages if you want. Which slices of the pie are getting more space in the circle than you want?

Then in the other circle, draw up your dream pie (in the sky). In your ideal world, what would be taking up the space in the circle? What would get the biggest piece of the pie?

Now ask yourself: *What would it take to change my life so that the bottom circle is my new reality?* What changes could—and would—you make to move toward that ideal use of your resources? What do you need to stop doing?

You can do the two-circle exercise for your money, your time, and your energy. Lots of people tell me this exercise has brought them lots of clarity about what they need to do to correct their courses.

You may look at your pie in the sky versus your current circumstances and feel completely discouraged. But the first step to getting your ship to the harbor you want is to define where you want to go. You can do this. Really. Just start. Knowing where you want to go and moving in that direction will be a source of lots of positivity in your life. There's nothing like seeing your destination on the horizon. And if you stay the course—the right course—you will get there. I'm sure of it!

The next three chapters of this book are focused on three specific practices that I believe are the keys God has given us to slow down and replace anger with love in our lives. These practices require space—emotional space and space in our schedules. But if you create the space for them, I guarantee you will love the results. These are time-tested practices that will set you free to love and be loved.

PART IV

Let It Go

13

Let It Go

Love keeps no record of wrongs....

—*1 Corinthians 13*

When my wife and I lived in Peru, I came face-to-face with a cultural norm that nearly drove me to insanity. Just behind our apartment there was a dirt alley where men—and women—would come to urinate on the wall. The alley was hidden enough that they could get some privacy from the street, but it was right outside my window. People peed all over that alley. Sometimes they even peed on our door. The owners of the apartments in our area put up a sign threatening people who urinated there, but at any hour of the day or night, you could look out our window and see someone squatting or standing—sometimes while looking right at the sign.

I got obsessed with stopping this behavior. (By now, you know I have control issues.) So I would sit by the window on the second floor like a crotchety old man and yell at people as they were unzipping or squatting. If I caught them in time, they'd normally lower their heads and run on. But sometimes I yelled too late, and they were already mid-stream, and you know how that goes.

I wish I could tell you that I eventually learned to laugh this off. But I didn't. I just kept yelling, thinking I could control and change an entire cultural norm. But it was a losing battle. In fact, I went back to that apartment in Peru last year, and the alley still smelled like urine. Ugh.

I still get irritated thinking about the injustice that went down in that alley. You'd think I would have let it go by now, but I haven't. And that's a real problem of mine. I have a really hard time letting some things go.

I'm guessing you do too.

I sincerely hope no one is peeing on your wall, but we all have experiences on a daily basis that irritate us. The off-handed comment your mother-in-law made. The flight booking mistake that cost you a ridiculous "service" fee. The people who bring twenty-seven items to the fifteen-items-only lane at the grocery store—and pay with a check—when you're in a hurry. I'm annoyed by people who don't use their blinkers. And don't even get me started on my thoughts about people in the airport talking on speaker phone while standing in the middle a moving walkway. (Not cool!) We've all got little annoyances that we spend tons of energy trying to fight.

Deep inside us we have a sense of justice that says, "It's just not right that _____." (You fill in the blank.)

It's not right how that person shows total disregard for every-one else.

It's not right that my car got hit in the parking lot, and the person drove off without leaving a note.

And those are just the little things. We've all got some big hurts and injustices from our past that we can add to the list. Some of us have major, life-altering events that left us wounded and angry.

It's not right that your ex got the better deal in the settlement.

It's not right what your father did to your family.

When a bunch of those "not rights" build up, they can lead to some major anger and resentment.

If you really want to walk in love and release your anger and anxiety, you'll have to get really good at learning to let it go at some point.

Love slows down to let it go.

Waiting for Your Happy Ending

A few days ago, my daughter had an emotional meltdown because she couldn't get a little toy box to close. She came to me all angry and in tears, saying, "Close it, Daddy! Close it!" The problem was that the box was damaged, and it wouldn't close completely. I just couldn't get her to understand that the box would never close perfectly.

My daughter is three.

I am in my forties.

I'm still learning the lesson I was trying to teach my daughter yesterday.

It's really easy to fall into thinking that everything in life can fit neatly together and give me the perfect ending I want if I just push hard enough. All the movies we watch and sermons we hear tend to tie a nice bow on all the drama. "And they all lived happily ever after with sunshine and unicorns." We start to believe that everything should end perfectly. We want our happily ever after, and we know what it should look like.

When I have a disagreement with my wife, I want her to come to my conclusion. I keep nagging or manipulating until she does. But she doesn't, and resentment builds. There are people who have hurt me that I'm convinced will come around and admit their guilt one day. But they don't. I obsess over my perfect ending. I won't back down until I get it. And it makes me miserable in the meantime.

Our world is broken. No matter how hard we push or manipulate for our happy ending, there are situations in life that will never fit together perfectly or end how we want them to end. There will be some things we never get closure on. We can't change the past. We can't change what happened. There are some things we're facing right now that we can't change. We can throw a fit, or we can accept this truth and work with what we have. When we embrace what is without stubbornly holding on to an obsession with everything being like we want it to be, then we can let it go. And letting it go creates space for love and peace to rule in our hearts and minds.

The Path to Glory

We live in a world filled with people. And when you hang around people, sooner or later you'll end up getting bumped into, mistreated, ignored, or just plain abused. There's no way around it. Again, there are some things we can't control. But there is always something we can control: our response to what happens.

That's why wise King Solomon said, "It's to one's glory to overlook an offense."[1] We're impressed with people who stay calm when they're being attacked or mistreated. We all love being around folks who don't take things personally or get upset at off-handed comments or slow drivers. Those are the kinds of people who are fun to be with. That's the glory Solomon is talking about. The ability to let go of the small things and not take them personally will make you stand out. It actually makes you look good. Nothing is quite as impressive as someone who can take a few hits and keep moving forward with a smile on their face.

Moving forward is what letting go is really all about. When you decide to let go, you're making a decision to move ahead and put the past behind you. All we have is today. What's done is done. Sure, it left a mark. It wasn't right that it happened. But we have to play with the cards life handed us. And here's the thing: when it comes to letting go of the past, we have to let go of both the negative and the positive. I'll talk more about the positive a little later, but first I want to talk about letting go of the negative parts of our past.

I know that many reading this have had some major, painful experiences in life. Abandonment. Betrayal. Rejection. Humiliation. I'm truly sorry for the bad things that happened. When I say you'll need to let it go, I'm not saying you need to simply overlook the injustice and act like it didn't affect you. You may need to have the courage to confront it or stand up and speak out. But here's the thing: If you confront the injustice from a place of resentment or bitterness, I can guarantee it won't go well. But if you can let go of the hurt, pain, and anger, it can give you strength to move forward from a place of love. The best way to live out of love is to keep a pure, clear heart.

Protect the Source

I took a Summit Leaders team rafting through the Grand Canyon a few years back. Our adventure started about two hours north of Flagstaff, Arizona. The Colorado River was crystal clear and fresh at the place we launched our rafting expedition. After a safety lesson and a few basic paddling tips, we set out on our six-day journey deep into the canyon. But about two miles into the trip, our guide pointed to the right. "Looks like the Paria is running," he said. "Say goodbye to the clear water."

I looked ahead and saw a stream of brown water flowing into our nice, clean river. The Paria is a seasonal stream that flushes tons of sediment from miles upstream right into the Colorado River. In no time, the entire river was brown and milky, and it stayed that way for the rest of the six-day trip. That one tiny stream miles upriver turned the mighty Colorado into a cloudy mess.

King Solomon said, "Above all else, guard your heart, for everything you do flows from it."[2] Our hearts are meant to be like a pure and clear stream. The purest love comes from a pure heart. But if we aren't careful, hurt and bitterness will pollute that stream. Offense, betrayal, disappointment, or failure can taint the pure waters of our hearts and leave us jaded and cynical. When we don't let go of those past offenses and hurt, they can quickly turn to resentment. The longer we hold on to the offenses, the more tainted the waters will be.

It can be hard to see when we've gotten jaded or cynical. We tell ourselves we're just cautious or trying to be realistic, but we often have unresolved hurt that is clouding our ability to see clearly. We don't see just how negative or cynical we've become—but others do. And being that way tends to repel people from wanting to be around us. It actually sabotages the very thing we want most—love.

Cynicism causes us to expect or look for the negative in every situation. Cynicism can ruin even the best of moments. It makes us question the motives and intentions of everyone around us. This leads to more anxiety, fear, and anger. It also makes us no fun to be around. But choosing to let go and not hold on to negative past experiences has a way of cleaning out the most tainted parts of our souls.

The World's Best Filter

I got altitude sickness the first time I climbed Mount Kilimanjaro. A big part of the reason I got sick was because I wasn't drinking enough water. Based on that experience, I'm always warning team members to drink lots of water. One of the most common causes of illness for people on my hiking teams is dehydration. Staying hydrated is imperative. But getting the water you need can be a challenge in nature. Depending on what's upstream, even the seemingly purest of water sources can be contaminated.

So when I lead a team, I bring a top-of-the-line water purification filter. It removes pretty much anything in the water that can harm you. I've pumped water from stagnant streams and not gotten sick. Those filters are expensive, but I purchase a new one for every trip. The price is absolutely worth it to make sure the team doesn't get hurt by unclean water. We sit around in a circle every night and take turns pumping pure water for the next day.

I wonder what could happen in our lives if we developed a daily habit of filtering out those little offenses that can build up and taint the clear, flowing streams of our hearts. What if every evening we processed what happened to us through our own filter of forgiveness and decided to not let the sun go down on our anger?

I wish letting go was as simple as just pumping a lever. Sometimes the hurt is so deep that letting it go can feel like giving up part of yourself. But it's possible to get to a place where your heart is free and clear from the effects of anger and hurt. You don't have to live with the weight of depression and anxiety that comes from holding on to what happened to you. You can let it go and start to live from a place of freedom. The past doesn't have to dominate your present or your future. You can break free from the power that hurt holds over you. You can get back to the joy of a clear, pure heart.

Forgiveness is the filter that clears out the hurt and anger in your heart.

In the famous words of Corrie ten Boom: "Forgiveness is the key that unlocks the door of resentment and the handcuffs of hatred." Letting go of the negative from our past always requires forgiveness. So let's take a closer look at how to let go through forgiveness. Because there's a good chance you may have believed a few lies about what it means to forgive.

14

Forgive

To love means loving the unlovable.
To forgive means pardoning the unpardonable.

—G.K. Chesterton

When I first started Summit Leaders, it was my side hustle. I worked as a music director at a church so I could keep a steady income, but I led trips on the side. One Sunday while I was on vacation, the senior pastor (a dear friend up to that point) offered my job to the guy filling in for me. He didn't even tell me. Another staff member told me what happened. I never saw it coming. And it stung. I was reeling for weeks. My wife and I left the church angry and confused. For months, I held on to resentment toward that pastor. I'd wake up at night thinking about the injustice. I'd fantasize about devious ways I could get revenge. (Hey, don't judge!)

That was a pretty dark season for me. It was a daily struggle. I remember thinking I never wanted to be in ministry again. I was convinced that every pastor out there was power-hungry and abusive. I felt betrayed by friends in the church who didn't come to my defense. I got really cynical. It wasn't until I learned what I'll share in this chapter that I was able to really forgive that pastor and move forward. Now I look back and am grateful for what happened. I wouldn't wish the experience on anyone, and I don't want to do it again, but without that experience, I doubt I'd be where I am today. I see that hurt through a new frame.

Which is why it's imperative that we take the time to look back at past hurts and negative experiences and choose to forgive. Our ability to love and be loved, now and in the future, hinges on our ability to forgive.

Love slows down to forgive.

The Price of Unforgiveness

A while back, I was recording some material about forgiveness and noticed the producer of the show smiling and nodding his head in agreement with what I was saying. During a break, he shared that many years earlier his sister had been shot in the head execution-style by her angry ex-husband. The man also shot the producer's father. Miraculously, both of them lived. The man was imprisoned, but he was released a short time later. The whole family lived in fear for months, wondering if that angry man was coming to try to kill them.

The producer shared how badly he wanted to repay this man for what he had done to his family. But he never acted on it. He just held in the anger. Shortly after all those horrible events, he began having medical issues that doctors weren't able to diagnose. It caused all sorts of physical problems for him. One day, he was talking to his pastor about the health issues and asking for prayer. The pastor asked him if there was someone in his life he might not have forgiven. He admitted that he still harbored huge amounts of resentment toward that man for what he had done to his family. The pastor walked him through the steps of forgiveness in a prayer. Amazingly, all his negative health symptoms quickly disappeared!

There is a growing amount of medical research showing a connection between physical health problems and holding on to unforgiveness. In one study, Charlotte vanOyen-Witvliet, a professor at Hope College, asked seventy-one college students to either think about an injustice done to them or to think about forgiving someone who had hurt them. She later wrote, "When focused on unforgiving responses, [the subjects'] blood pressure surged, their heart rates increased, brow muscles tensed, and negative feelings escalated." But "by contrast, forgiving responses induced calmer feelings and physical responses." She concluded that "harboring unforgiveness comes at an emotional and a physiological cost. Cultivating forgiveness may cut these costs."[1]

In both Spanish and French, the word *sentir* means "to feel." When we "re-sent," we feel the pain of the hurt over and over. If we don't let go of resentment, it can have some disastrous results. Ongoing resentment has the potential to hurt us worse than the original hurt. Resentment builds when we hold on to past injustices and keep reliving them in our minds.

When resentment grows, anger builds. Our anger can turn into an out-of-control wildfire. It can get to a point where we just want to watch the whole world burn. Anyone who resembles the person who hurt us becomes a target for our anger. We may harbor anger at an entire race, gender, or society all because of something one person did to us. The pain becomes our obsession as we keep reliving the hurt.

Thinking about the same thing over and over in your mind is called "ruminating." The word *ruminate* has two meanings: 1) to think deeply about something, and 2) to bring up and chew again what has already been chewed and swallowed. Cows and sheep are ruminants. They keep eating the same food over and over again by chewing it, swallowing it, then heaving it back up into their mouths and chewing it some more. Yum, right?

Ruminating on hurt and negative thoughts is like chewing the same disgusting food over and over. In the words of one psychologist, "Rumination is the mental-health bad boy. It's associated with almost everything bad in the mental health field—obsessive-compulsive disorder, anxiety, depression ... probably hives too."[2] Resentment is ruminating on hurts and injustices from the past. It doesn't change the past. It doesn't make the person who hurt you want to change. The only person it's hurting is you. It's like drinking poison and thinking the person who hurt you will die.

When Peter asked how many times he had to forgive someone who hurt him, Jesus told a parable about a man who owed a king an enormous amount of money. The king called him in and told him it was time to pay. The guy didn't have the money, so he begged for leniency. The king forgave his entire debt. The man was elated. But as he was heading back home, he ran into a guy who owed him a tiny amount of money compared to what he had just been forgiven. The guy who was just forgiven the huge debt threw the other man into prison until he could pay him back. Word got back to the king, who called the guy he forgave back in. He was angry. He said, "You wicked servant ... I canceled all that debt of yours because you begged me to. Shouldn't you have had mercy on your fellow servant just as I had on you?"[3] Then he turned the man over to jailers to be tortured.

Torture. That's exactly what it starts to feel like when you think over and over again about what that person, church, or organization did to you. It can ruin your sleep. It can ruin your day. It can even ruin your health. But forgiveness sets you free from the torture of resentment. The good news is that forgiveness isn't complicated. It can be hard, but it's not complicated. But often we're held back from getting free through forgiveness because we've believed some untruths about what forgiving really means. Let me explain.

The Myths of Forgiveness

Forgiveness is a decision. After that pastor hurt me, I had to get serious about making a decision to forgive him. But before I could truly let go of the hurt, I had to correct some wrong ideas I had about for-giveness. Based on my own personal experience and what I've learned walking others through letting go of hurt, here are a few myths (dare I say "lies"?) that we've believed or been told about forgiveness.

Myth 1: I can forgive once they admit what they did.

Jesus debunked this myth and gave us a great example. As He was dying, He said, "Father forgive them for they do not know what they are doing."[4] He forgave before anyone even realized they needed it. You may never hear a confession from the people who've hurt you. They may never choose to acknowledge their guilt. If the person who hurt you is a parent who has passed away or a criminal who was never caught, it's simply not possible to seek a confession. In many cases, it's dangerous and unwise to confront the person who hurt you.

The great news is, you don't need the other person to acknowledge their guilt before you can forgive them. The power is in your hands right here and now. Forgiveness is your choice. It has nothing to do with whether or not the other person admitted their guilt. You don't have to wait for them. You were a victim of someone hurting you, but don't stay a victim. Don't let victimhood be your identity. You are way more than what happened to you. You have power to break free from being a victim by letting go and forgiving right now—even if they never admit what they did.

Myth 2: I'll know when it's time to forgive. It'll feel right.

I hate to break it to you, but that feeling is never going to come. This would be equivalent to deciding to get into shape and saying, "I'll just know when it's time to go to the gym. I'll feel it." Not likely. There will always be other, more appealing options—like nursing your wounds and continuing to think about the bad things that person did to you. The truth is, the feeling will follow the action. You'll get the positive feelings you're looking for only after you choose to forgive. And even then, it might take some time, but trust me, it will come. Right now is always the right time to forgive.

Myth 3: Forgive and forget.

Let me be blunt: You cannot forgive and forget. It is impossible. Your mind is too powerful to simply forget. It always remembers. If you spend your life trying to forget a hurt, thinking this is true forgiveness, you'll live in constant guilt and condemnation. We don't forgive and forget; we forgive and choose to remember with forgiveness.

Steps to Forgiveness

Forgiveness starts by admitting, "I was hurt."

That's hard to admit. I've walked emotionally strong, powerful men and women through forgiveness. They seem invincible. But when I ask them to say that they were hurt—out loud—their voices will crack. Sometimes they even start crying. Admitting vulnerability is not a good feeling. I don't want to admit that anyone had enough power to actually hurt me. But once you get up the courage to admit you were hurt, you've cracked open the door to being able to forgive.

The next step is to admit *how* you were hurt. Admit the need that wasn't met. Admit what was taken from you. You have to actually name the hurt. *I was betrayed. I was lied to. I was abandoned. I was disrespected. I was rejected.* You need to say it out loud to yourself. If you want, you can use the following as an example of what to say:

Name of person betrayed my trust and used it to take advantage of me. He hurt me.

Name of person lied to me and then told lies about me. She hurt me.

Name of person betrayed my family's trust. He hurt my family.

Name of person abandoned me. The person who should have protected me left me alone to fend for myself.

This is an intense process. So I don't recommend doing it alone. If the hurt is really deep or you've been holding on to it for a long time, ask a pastor or professional counselor who understands forgiveness to walk through it with you. When I chose to forgive the pastor who gave my job away, a friend who is a counselor helped me walk through it.

After I confessed my hurt and what I lost, she told me to repeat the ways that pastor had hurt me—but she had me add one final statement at the end: "But I choose to forgive him for hurting me."

It was awkward to say it all out loud again. But the relief I felt was amazing. It was like I regained a sense of hope and perspective. I wasn't a victim. I was choosing to forgive someone who had hurt me. It was my choice. More importantly, I was embracing God's grace to forgive, and that released peace into my life.

The final step in the forgiveness process is this: *Remind yourself of your decision.* Remind yourself when you wake up. Remind yourself when you think about what the person did. Remind yourself before you go to bed. You'll know you've truly forgiven that person when you look back at the hurt and feel no anger or resentment—only peace. Forgiveness always leads to inner peace. You may have been holding on to the past for so long that you can't even imagine what that kind of peace would feel like. But know this: It's yours for the taking. You can have this peace. It can start right now when you choose to forgive. When you forgive, slowly and surely, you'll experience a deep peace that goes beyond anything we can explain. When that peace takes root, you'll have begun to really heal.

15

Heal

Healing doesn't mean the damage never existed.
It means the damage no longer controls our lives.

—*Unknown Author*

A few years ago, I had a team member sprain his ankle on the third day of a multi-day hike. I could tell from his swollen ankle that he was experiencing a lot of pain. But he was a tough guy, so he pushed through and kept walking on it. Our local guide was not happy about this decision. He told me we needed to hoist him up on a stretcher and carry him to the next camp. Of course, the guy who was injured didn't want the embarrassment of being hauled down the trail on a stretcher. So when I suggested what the guide wanted, he kept limping along, telling me, "I'm fine, really. It doesn't even hurt."

I believed him and waved off the guide's offer. "He said he's fine."

The guide shot back a frustrated look. "Yes, but that's because he's still moving. His body is compensating. That will wear off tonight when he slows down. Tomorrow he's going to be in bad shape. I'll have the stretcher ready."

Sure enough, the next morning, the injured young man told me there was no way he could complete the hike. So we called the stretcher, and for the rest of the trip, eight men took turns carrying him along the treacherous trail. The guy who hurt his ankle on that hike was, without a doubt, the most in-shape person on the trip. He had won a national contest that required massive physical stamina. But it doesn't matter how strong you are: if you don't take time to slow down and heal from a hurt, you'll either make the hurt worse or re-injure yourself.

We all run the same risk when it comes to pain in our lives. When we forgive, we set ourselves free from what was done to us. But if we never give ourselves time to heal, we run the risk of creating even more pain. We have to slow down and take the proper steps to heal.

Love slows down to heal.

The Pain That Won't Go Away

A while back, I was talking with a lady who had been separated from her husband for over a year and was just about to sign the final paperwork for the divorce. She mentioned in passing that she had been dating a man for the entire year she had been separated. I wanted to be happy for her, but I was concerned. "Do you think it would be wise to take some time to process what just happened before you jump back into another relationship?"

Without hesitation she said, "Oh, the marriage has been over for years. It's just a matter of paperwork now." She said she wanted to put the past behind her and move on. I'm all in favor of moving on, but I've seen that if we don't take time to heal from a wound, we are very likely to reopen that wound and bleed on people who didn't hurt us.

Or we just keep walking into more and more hurt.

Sadly, that's exactly what happened to her. She has bounced from one abusive relationship to another since that divorce. It hurts to watch. She's a wonderful person with lots of love to give, but she has a deep hurt that never had time to fully heal. It's like she's swimming around with a bleeding wound. That wound attracts a lot of attention, but it's mostly from sharks who prey on her woundedness. The more it happens, the more angry and bitter she becomes. Unhealed hurts tend to drive us back into patterns in relationships that always end the same way. More deep hurt.

We've all been hurt. We all need some healing. Sometimes the hurts happen early in life. Our parents have their own hurts that can easily be passed on to us. Parents who are overly critical or don't give their children the time or attention they need can leave a lasting impact. I work with guys all the time who are still trying to prove themselves to a father who isn't even alive anymore. Lots of them ruin their marriages, taking jobs that require too much time away, all trying to show their dad they are "manly enough."

If you had a parent who set impossible standards, you might have a wound of feeling like you're never enough. Some parents demand a level of perfection in looks or academic performance that is more a reflection of the parent's own issues than the child's. More often than not, that parent didn't take the time to work through their own issues and get some healing, and they unintentionally passed it on to their child. It's not disloyal to admit your parents made some mistakes that hurt you. The most loving thing you can do to fix it is to acknowledge the hurt then do your best to heal—because no matter how good your intentions are, if you don't get your own healing, you'll inevitably pass your pain on to others. But you can stop it. You can break the cycle. Slowing down to heal is how you can make sure you don't pass pain on to those you love most.

The Spiral of Healing

Healing takes time. And time is something we don't feel like we have a lot of. The older we get, the more we feel our time is limited. We may even feel the need to make up for lost time. So we end up racing ahead, still wounded, trying to get the security, connection, and control that was lost. But once you've made the decision to forgive, it's really important that you slow down and take the time needed to properly heal. Forgiveness sets you free—right now. But healing is a process. It involves grieving what you lost.

You've probably heard of the five stages of grief: denial, anger, bargaining, depression, and acceptance. Because they're called stages, it's easy to think grief is a linear process. Stage One, Two, Three … *Click*. "Yeah! I'm over it!" But grieving isn't like that. It's more like a spiral. The pain tends to loop back around. You may wake up days, months, or years later and be hit by a wave of sadness and anger that feels just as intense as the moment the hurt happened. This doesn't mean you haven't truly forgiven. It just means you need to remind yourself that you chose to forgive.

The good news is, the spiral will get wider and wider. The episodes will get further and further apart. If the spiral comes back around again, don't feel guilty. It's normal. Just remind yourself that you chose to forgive. Eventually, you'll get to a place where the memory of the event will only bring peace. Again, we don't forgive and forget. We forgive and remember with forgiveness.

Let the Healing Begin

If you've ever broken a bone, you know that a properly healed bone is actually stronger than it was before the break. But the bone has to be set to heal correctly—which means you have to slow down, give it time, and stop putting stress on it. You have to take pressure off so the healing can happen.

How long does it take to heal? Well, that's tricky. It'll be different for each person and situation. I think you'll know you are on the path to healing when you're willing to take the time to evaluate exactly what happened and what lessons you learned as honestly as possible. Remember, experience isn't the best teacher; *evaluated* experience is the best teacher.

There's a fascinating verse that says Jesus learned obedience through what he suffered.[1] The idea that Jesus would need to learn anything might seem confusing. I'm sure there's lots of deep theology that's above my pay grade in that passage, but the fact is, Jesus learned through suffering and pain. We are no different. Your pain has taught you something. But you won't get the full value of it until you do the homework of cementing what you've learned into a new framework. Don't assume you won't make the same mistakes again. People make the same mistakes all the time, mostly because they never slowed down to evaluate what really happened.

We have to get honest about what happened. We have to take responsibility for any part we played in the painful situation. When that pastor hurt me, it took me a long time to admit it, but the truth was that I wasn't giving that job the energy it required. I was so focused on building the outdoor-adventure side hustle that I was neglecting parts of my job. The pastor saw this. He handled it incorrectly, but I'm pretty sure it was the main reason he felt the need to let me go. It took me a long time to admit my part in the situation. Admitting our responsibility can be painful. But to keep from making the same mistakes again, we need to admit the truth.

Seeing clearly can be challenging. It might require some outside insight. Because we're so close to our lives, we have blind spots that can keep us from seeing things as they really are. It's easy to develop overly simple, fear-based explanations that actually keep us from truly being able to love. One man told me he was never going to marry someone who was the same race as his first wife because "those people are crazy." I pointed out that there are crazy people in every race and ethnicity. We're all just humans with issues. If he wrote off everyone who resembled his ex-wife in any way, he might unintentionally miss out on the loving person God had for his future.

A wrong mindset can lead to improper healing. A broken bone that is set in the wrong position will grow back contorted. Sometimes it takes a little pain to reset the bone into the right position. The same is true of our emotional healing. It might hurt before it gets better. It might hurt a little to acknowledge some truths about ourselves and the situation. We have to make sure that our perspective is set correctly about what happened, or we may move forward with a contorted view of life. That improper view can limit our ability to give and receive love. But when we heal—with truth as our guide, facing reality—we actually get stronger.

Stronger Than Before

A person with experience is never at the mercy of a person with a theory. When you've lived through a difficult situation and have chosen to move forward, you know a thing or two about how to make it in hard times. If you handle the challenge correctly, you will grow and be better for it. There are some things that can only be learned through bumps and bruises. A.W. Tozer once said, "It's doubtful whether God can use a man greatly, until He has wounded him deeply."[2] Pain teaches us. But too often, for obvious reasons, we want to run from pain.

Sometimes we need to just sit in the reality of the pain for a while. Rather than run from it or try to numb the pain, we need to let it do its work. Give yourself time to heal—even if it hurts a lot. Take steps to work through what actually happened. For some, this may mean (if it's safe) facing your fear and going back to the place you've been avoiding—the house, the town. It may be part of the reframing we talked about a few chapters ago. Do whatever it takes to symbolically let it go.

One pastor who had been unjustly fired by a church told me he felt he needed to burn a bunch of the angry letters that he and the board had exchanged during that painful separation. He made sure not to destroy those notes while he was angry. That would have just fed his anger. Instead, he waited to make sure that in his heart he had really forgiven. He also burned the copies of the minutes from the board meeting in which he had been slandered and shamed. The letters and notes were full of lies and justifications about why these men believed they were doing the right thing. Burning those papers in a field was his final act of letting it go. He did his best to let it go from a pure heart, untainted by bitterness.

After I talked about forgiveness at a marriage group, a man told me that for years he couldn't drive past a certain hotel because that was where he had found his wife cheating on him. Every day, he drove way out of his way to avoid passing that specific hotel. The memory of that pain represented by that hotel controlled him. It limited him. He had forgiven his wife, and their marriage had been reconciled for years, but he still had a hard time truly letting go. His act of healing was to finally drive past that hotel.

One of the quickest ways to decide what action you need to take is to ask yourself: *How would I respond to that person if I truly had forgiven and let it go?*

Then go do that.

The feeling will follow the action. Be patient with yourself. Healing takes time. But if you choose to forgive, you will heal. You will get strong again. Probably stronger than before. You'll be back on your feet in no time. You'll be wiser and more open to give and receive love than before because you'll have learned what real love is about—forgiveness. Once you have truly forgiven, you can truly let go of the pain and embrace the life you have. You can accept what is.

16

Accept What Is

We must let go of the life we have planned,
so as to accept the one that is waiting for us.

—Joseph Campbell

There's a world map hanging on the wall in our living room with little white pins stuck in places my wife and I have visited. About half of those pins represented places I visited before we were married. I spent three years leading backpacking teams all over the world right out of college. In my months off from leading teams, I just kept traveling. I went scuba diving in the Great Barrier Reef. Backpacking in Europe. Cliff diving in the Caribbean. Slept in a yurt on the Mongolian steppe. Rappelled off the Great Wall of China. I was going nonstop, trying to soak up life as much as I could. Nothing seemed impossible or too hard. I would take on any challenge and go at it full force.

Sometimes when I look at my life now, I feel like half the man I used to be. I'm married, have a daughter, and have many more responsibilities now. I struggle with lots of fear because I have lots to lose. All that responsibility has slowed me down and made me more cautious. Sometimes when I'm overwhelmed, I find my mind drifting back to those good ol' days and wishing I could have some of them back. I'll flip through old pictures or look at a map and retrace the trips I took.

I love my life now, but it's really easy to compare it to the way it used to be—back in the simpler, good ol' days. That kind of thinking can quickly lead to frustration and resentment. The reality is, the past I'm comparing to my present isn't the full picture. I remember the glory days and forget the bad parts. When I'm honest, I have to admit I was really lonely much of the time I was traveling. I wondered if I would ever get married. At times I wondered if I fit in with "normal people." I remember the glory but forget the emotional turmoil.

Such is the nature of the past. It can really mess with your ability to embrace the now. Letting go of the negative experiences and pain of the past is one thing. But not all of life is pain. Sometimes the greatest challenge to moving forward is sentimentality—being constantly focused on an idealized past. If we get too hung up in the past, we will never be able to embrace the present, the reality of what is right in front of us.

Love slows down to accept what is.

Rosy Retrospection

Recently, I was looking at some pictures I took while camping on the Great Wall of China. They're pretty glamorous. But what those pictures don't reflect is the fact that half my team came woefully unprepared for the conditions on that hike. I ended up giving my tent and sleeping bag to a few of the team members, and I spent the coldest night of my life sleeping out under the stars. It was miserable. I was delirious while we were rappelling off the wall the next morning. But the pictures don't show that. They just show me smiling and looking all hardcore.

We're all prone to something psychologists call "rosy retrospection"—remembering the past as better than it actually was. Our minds filter out the bad and remember the good. One study showed that the older we get, the more our brains remember the positive.[1] It's wonderful to remember the past fondly. But comparing the present to an idealized past can create discouragement, depression, and resentment.

Which is probably why King Solomon said, "Do not say, 'Why were the old days better than these?' For it is not wise to ask such questions."[2] It's not wise to compare the present with the past because we're prone to leave out the negative parts. Remember, most of life is about interpretation and perspective. When we look back at the "old days" as perfection, it can lead to discontentment with our current situation. I talk to lots of church and business leaders who like to reflect back on the glory days of their churches or businesses. Often they're seeing a decline in attendance or sales and don't know what to do about it. They compare current employees or congregants to their fantasy of the past and just become frustrated. Your present will rarely be as wonderful as your idealized past. This happens in lots of marriages too. Seasons of marriage change, and comparing the current season to the way it used to be leads to discontentment. We have to learn to appreciate the past but live in the present reality of what is.

The Apostle Paul had a pretty solid and diverse resume. He went to the best schools and ran with some of the most influential people of his day. He had some pretty high points in his past, but he also had a few things that easily could have haunted him. Before his conversion, he was responsible for killing Christians. But Paul put it all in perspective. In one letter, he shared his mindset: "One thing I do: forgetting what lies behind and straining forward to what lies ahead...."[3] Paul wasn't gonna hang his hat on his past—good, bad, or ugly. And he wasn't going to let his past limit him. Neither should we.

Moving Forward

I've been hanging around church for over forty years now, and I have seen that holding on to the idealized past can cause some serious anger and resentment. Nowhere is this more blatant than in church wars. I've watched wonderful, godly men and women who turn into raging cage fighters when someone wants to change a music style or update the way a church does something. A few years back, I watched as a once vibrant church began a slow decline. They hired a new pastor, but within two years, the congregants got upset for one reason or another with the pastor's changes and fired him. This cycle happened over and over. They would spend months looking for another pastor, and attendance would further decline. Eventually, they got to a place where they had to decide whether to hire a pastor or keep their building. They voted to keep the building. With no pastor, the attendance declined more. It was sad to watch.

What's crazy is, this church was sitting on millions of dollars of prime real estate. They could have sold the property, built a smaller building, and had enough money in the bank to pay a pastor for the rest of their lives. And they knew it. But they were so attached to a building that they refused to let it go. And I understand why. That building is where their children grew up—Sunday schools, church events. It held a lot of good memories and sentimentality for those folks. Those days were long gone, but the folks just couldn't bring themselves to release what used to be. The wonderful past undermined that church's ability to continue ministering to the community. Eventually, they were forced to sell. But before it got to that point, lots of lifelong relationships ended in fighting and anger and hurt. All over a silly old building!

I think that's why Jesus said that you can't put new wine into old wineskins.[4] Back in the day, wine was held in dried animal skins. But after a while, the old wineskins got brittle and hard. New wine is always expanding. It will push and press. If the container isn't flexible or doesn't leave room for growth, it will break. Real love is constantly expanding and welcoming the new. If we get too attached to an old framework or how it used to be, we're prone to miss what God wants to do now. Or worse, we might just become angry and resentful over the new work—not realizing that it's actually God's work.

God never changes, but He often works in new, creative ways. We can't get hung up on our ideal of how things should be based on how they were in the past. We have to be willing to embrace what is—right now.

I've had lots of parents ask me to intervene in conflicts they're having with their kids. They want their kids to follow in their footsteps by taking over the family business, going to a certain school, or pursuing a certain path in life. They had a positive experience, and they want their kids to have one too. So they pressure and manipulate their kids. They hold on to their ideal so strongly that they create division. They really want what they believe to be best for their kids, but they end up forcing their children to be replicas of themselves. But their kids aren't *them*. They are unique. Trying to force them into a mold that isn't who they are will just make them (and you) frustrated and angry.

If you have control issues like me, I know this is hard to believe, but there is freedom in facing the reality of who our kids are, what our life really is, and who we really are. I'm not saying you need to accept it all passively. Some of your reality probably needs to change. But you'll be able to change it from a place of love when you let go of your expectations and ideals and embrace what is. And for the things that can't change into what you want them to be, you can find a lot of peace by choosing to embrace what is and receiving God's grace for right now. God knows your situation, and He has the grace you need to walk in peace, right where you are.

There's a burden and a blessing for every season. Shoulder the burden and embrace the blessing. Stay flexible. Never stop learning. Don't hold too tightly to sentimental ideals of what it "should be." Embrace what God is doing right now. The reality of what He is doing now is what opens the door for you to find a place of mental peace and stillness—a place of solitude.

PART V

Seek Solitude

Seek Solitude

Solitude is the place where we can connect
with profound bonds that
are deeper than the emergency bonds
of fear and anger.

—Henri Nouwen

Right out of college, I took a team on a four-month backpacking trip through Asia. We started in Hong Kong, worked our way up to Beijing, up through the steppes and deserts of Mongolia, back down through far-western China, and ultimately up to Tibet with a visit to Mount Everest. We were moving nonstop for several months, crossing the country. China has a population of more than 1.3 billion people, and much of the industrial part of the country runs at a frenetic pace. There's construction going literally twenty-four hours of the day in the cities. On the trains, you're cramped together with thousands of other people. Since personal space isn't really a value in a very communal society, you can be sure that someone is always going to be trying to practice English with you or just curiously poking around in your stuff as you travel.

Which is what made Mount Everest so unique. It's the quietest, most desolate place I've ever been. We arrived late in the afternoon and stayed in a guest house at what is said to be the highest Buddhist monastery in the world. It's right at the foot of the Rongbuk Glacier that runs along the north face of Everest. Our hosts prepared yak-meat stew and yak-butter tea for dinner. I didn't sleep much that night because of the seventeen-thousand-foot altitude and the bitter cold. We set out early the next morning. As we hiked, the team started to spread out—some hiking faster than others. At one point, I looked up and realized I was all alone. No wildlife. No people. From time to time, I'd hear the crack of ice somewhere around me as the sun did its best to melt the permafrost. But other than that, it was absolutely silent. I'm not sure I've had that much silence since.

Even though it was quiet all around me, chaos was inside my head. My mind was spinning with travel plans, money concerns, and what it would be like when I got home. It was hard to enjoy the moment because I just couldn't get my mind to shut off or calm down.

I know I'm not alone in this. For most of us, even if you manage to find a quiet place or moment, getting your mind to calm down is a whole other challenge. People tell me, "I just can't get my mind to shut off." Noise is everywhere—inside our heads and around us. Screens and music are always playing; kids, barking dogs, and conversations can even turn our own homes into pretty noisy places. Some of us have gotten so used to the noise that we get nervous when it's not there. Noise becomes comforting. If it gets too quiet, we quickly grab our phone or turn on the TV to fill in the awkward silence.

Noise drives more noise. The cumulative effect of noise can build into tension and anxiety. What's urgent always seems to be loudest, and some of us can't ever escape the noise of the urgent. Breaking news, flash sales, reminders on our phones, text messages. We aren't made to be constantly stimulated. It leads to lots of anxiety. We need moments of peace and quiet. Fortunately, there's a powerful practice that can help ensure that the noise doesn't push you into overdrive.

That practice is solitude. Seeking solitude can help you regain a sense of peace in your mind.

Love slows down to seek solitude.

Strength through Solitude

Solitude is mental stillness.

That's my definition, not the dictionary's. I use that definition because, for many of us, it's just not possible to be physically alone or far from the madding crowd on a regular basis. Being by yourself is optimal for solitude, and we do need to carve out time to just be alone, but just being alone doesn't necessarily mean you'll get any mental stillness. Fortunately, you can train yourself to get still in your mind and find peace no matter what's happening around you. You can get the benefits of solitude, even if you can't physically remove yourself from the chaos.

Thomas Merton was a monk who offered some serious encouragement for those of us who don't have the option of hiding in a cave or a cottage in the mountains. He said, "As soon as a man is fully disposed to be alone with God, he is alone with God no matter where he may be—in the country, the monastery, the woods, or the city."[1] Mental stillness can happen anywhere. But it takes some practice. It's exercise and training for your spirit.

In Isaiah 30:15, God tells Israel, "In repentance and rest is your salvation, in quietness and trust is your strength" (NIV). This statement seems really counterintuitive. In physical exercise, the harder you push and stretch your muscles, the stronger you get. No pain, no gain. But God says that spiritual strength comes from the total opposite action. It comes from quietness and trust. "Be still and know that I am God."[2]

Stillness is strength.

But in this world driven by fear and anger, with everyone trying to get their needs met and achieve their hopes and dreams, stillness and quietness won't just happen. You'll have to create space for solitude. The good news is, you have time for solitude. But there's a good chance the noise of the urgent has convinced you that you don't.

We Have Time; We Need Focus

In 2018, the average Internet user spent 144 minutes each day browsing social media.[3] That's over two hours each day. Spending two hours a day on anything—whether for entertainment or work—means it's a serious value. You may not spend two hours scrolling through social media, but I'm sure you spend at least some time watching TV or listening to music. We all have time. But often we don't realize just how much time and mental space we're giving to electronic media. The gods of the Internet have figured out how to keep you watching, listening, or scrolling. In fact, social media is built on the same psychology that gets people hooked on slot machines. Getting likes, shares, or mentions pays out intermittent surges of adrenaline that keep you coming back for more. The more you scroll, the more social media companies can place ads in front of you that lead to big money for them.[4]

Don't get me wrong. I love social media as much as the next person, and I can easily slip into a scrolling binge when I'm tired or bored or anxious. It has a numbing effect. It can even feel like leisure. If I don't want to call it leisure, I can justify it by saying it's a good way to stay in contact with the people I love. But looking for that little surge of dopamine that comes on social media can become addictive. I can't tell you how many times I've found myself mindlessly opening apps or looking at flash sales just because I'm bored. My goal in saying this isn't to attack entertainment as evil; it's just a clear example of how we do have time for what we want. Entertainment is usually the path of least resistance. We do it without thinking.

We often don't see the direct results of all the time we spend on social media or entertainment. But the cumulative effects of it add up. Little by little, comparing our life to others' lives, reading articles about all the bad things that are happening out there, and just filling our minds with more information than we can handle starts to overload us. It makes our mind restless. Like an addictive drug, we just need a little more. It creates anxiety.

But when you begin to see the benefits of solitude, you'll get hooked on it too. But first, you have to get intentional about redirecting your habit of filling every spare moment with media and instead begin to develop a habit of seeking mental space and stillness.

Intentional Solitude

Unless you live in a monastery or a tent in the Rocky Mountains, I'm guessing that right about now you're thinking, *Solitude sounds great and all, but I don't have time to check out mentally.* We've got jobs, bills to pay, kids to care for, and relationships that require maintenance. You may not have the luxury of spending hours on end in nature or total silence, but you can create small moments of mental stillness right where you are. You just have to be intentional about it.

Here are some practical steps to get you started on making solitude a part of your value system:

1. Make it a priority. We give our resources to what we value. So the key is to start realizing there really is value in solitude. If you aren't convinced it has value, then I'm gonna ask you to just trust me for now. Just take a small step and see what happens. That small step of solitude will look different for each person. In our loud world, it probably won't mean total silence. But that's OK—you can still get the benefits if you choose to make it a priority. An attorney in my coaching program decided to start packing his lunch rather than going out to a restaurant. He'd eat, then he'd slip into a church near his office and spend time in prayer over lunch. That was his little moment of solitude, right in the middle of each day. He missed the social aspect of eating out, but he loved the benefits of having time to process his thoughts alone. (It also saved him loads of money.) You may not have the luxury of getting out of the house or office, but there are still opportunities. Drive to work with the radio off. Get to work a little early, hide your phone, and just sit in your car silently. Spend the last few hours of every evening in quiet rather than looking at a screen.

2. Set a realistic, attainable goal. Set yourself some small goals. When you accomplish small goals, you build momentum. You start to see that bigger goals are possible. I've set way too many lofty solitude goals. "I'm going to sit in silence for thirty minutes every day!" I may pull it off for two days, but then I miss a day. I feel guilty and figure I'll make it up the following day. I rarely do. Instead, I just give up all together. Don't do that! Give yourself a fighting chance. Aim low. Start with something reasonable and small. Five to ten dedicated minutes of no distraction with phones or people. Just see how it goes. Take small steps.

3. Silence the monkeys. Once you commit to pursuing moments of mental stillness, the next challenge is what Henri Nouwen describes as "calming the monkeys jumping in the banana trees." A few years back, one of my adventure teams camped in the jungle ruins of Yaxha, an unexcavated Mayan city. A family of howler monkeys was pretty upset about our being there. They groaned and screamed for hours. It wasn't until late in the night that they finally calmed down, and we were able to get some peace and quiet.

When you start to practice solitude, there will probably be some "monkeys" howling in your head. Worries about family. Job stuff. The leaking faucet. Keep a pen handy to write down what you need to remember or address later. But once you've written those things down, put them out of your mind and get back to stillness. If you're serious about it, the monkeys will eventually quiet down. It gets easier over time.

4. Trust the process. There will be days when you set time aside, go through the motions, and feel like nothing happened. It may feel like wasted time. Not every experience in solitude will be some life-changing event. But we have to learn to trust the process of what solitude builds in us over time. Just as noise has a cumulative effect, so does silence. In fact, one study shows that silence can actually build brain cells.[5] The fact that it seems like nothing is happening in solitude doesn't mean nothing is happening. It's just happening on a higher level.

Stephen Covey talks about "The Law of the Farm," which is based on something Jesus said. "The Kingdom of God is like a farmer who scatters seed on the ground. Night and day, while he's asleep or awake, the seed sprouts and grows, but he does not understand how it happens."[6] That's the law of the farm. The harvest doesn't pop up overnight. It has to grow. It starts small, then grows into its full potential.

And so do our spiritual lives. You probably won't realize it while it's happening, but slowly and surely, your anger, anxiety, and hurry will lessen. You just won't feel quite as stressed. The constant feeling of something hanging over your head will lighten. I don't know exactly how it happens, but it has worked for thousands of years and for countless numbers of people, and it will work for you. And it won't be because you exerted more effort; it will be because you chose to focus your energy and attention in the right direction. It's a slow work.

You can't buy the results of solitude in a pre-packaged meal kit. It won't be delivered to your door hot and ready to consume. You have to actually tend the farm that will produce the resources you are looking for. It will be slow. At times, it may feel like it takes an eternity. But if you invest the time, you'll eventually get to eat fruit from the trees of solitude you planted in your heart and mind. You'll find a new sense of love and wonder growing within you. And it will be really, really good.

Once you've decided to seek the discipline of solitude, there are some really specific exercises you can practice to help you get started. And that's what we'll talk about next—the exercises you can incorporate from a place of solitude that will help you release anger, anxiety, and hurry and trade them in for a sense of love, joy, peace, patience, kindness, goodness, gentleness, and self-control.

Breathe

*When you own your breath, no one can
steal your peace.*

—Unknown

The first time I climbed Mount Kilimanjaro, I got acute mountain sickness (AMS) and had to be rushed back down the night before we were supposed to summit. I was in my early twenties and in the best shape of my life. I had trained hard. But what I didn't realize was that strength is only part of the equation in mountain climbing.

The higher up you climb, the thinner the oxygen gets. That's why really high mountains take days to climb. It's not a distance thing; it's an altitude and oxygen thing. Each day you climb a little higher, then you come back down and camp at an altitude slightly lower than where you climbed to that day. You breathe as deeply as you can and drink lots of water to get oxygen into your system. This gives your body time to acclimatize to the changing oxygen levels. You have to be serious about making sure you're getting the air you need.

You may not be planning to climb Kilimanjaro, but I'm certain there are some mountains in your life right now that are cleaning your clock—the work project, the divorce, the problems with your child. They might even be making you feel nervous or nauseous. You only have so much control over your environment, but there is one thing you can control—yourself. You can find solitude and peace in the middle of even the hardest climbs. It sounds way too easy, but I believe that one of the simplest things you can do to bring peace in anxiety and anger is to breathe correctly. There's a connection between our physical body and our mental and emotional state. When you breathe correctly (I'll explain "correctly" in a minute), you actually set a course for peace in your mind and emotions.

Love slows down to breathe.

The Breath of God

Ever since experiencing a growth spurt in high school, I haven't been able to touch my toes. I stopped trying for many years. I concluded I'm just not flexible. But I injured my hip recently and had to find stretching exercises to improve my flexibility. Someone recommended yoga. I laughed at first. Not my style—I like lifting weights. But after hearing multiple medical professionals tell me it would help my flexibility, I went for it. I found a yoga class that was focused on exercise rather than chanting or connecting with the universe.

I'm in decent shape physically, but the first class was humiliating. I couldn't do half the exercises because I had such poor flexibility in my muscles. After class, the peppy instructor, who was in her seventies and in way better shape than me, pulled me aside and said, "You need to get your breathing right."

Breathing? I'm working on flexibility here, lady.

She walked me through a few stretches. When I got to what I thought was the full extent of my flexibility, she told me, "Now, breathe in deeply. As you exhale, push a little further." To my surprise, it worked. Little by little my flexibility started improving. When I think I'm stuck, I breathe deeply, then push a little more into the stretch.

The simple act of breathing can help stretch us on a spiritual level too. Breathing correctly has a way of pushing us deeper into a place of focus and solitude. The ancient Greek word *pneuma* (said *noo*-mah) can literally be translated as "breath." But it also means "spirit." That linguistic clue seems to indicate that we've known for a long time there's a connection between breath and spirit. The Genesis story of creation says God breathed into Adam to bring him to life.[1] Is it possible that breathing is actually a spiritual act that can help us reconnect with a power greater than ourselves? I tend to think it is. I wonder what could happen in our lives if we began to see each breath we take as a reminder of God's sustaining power in our lives? I'm pretty certain we'd feel a lot more mental stillness.

Breathing is the most basic thing we do to stay alive. You can stop eating and drinking for a while without serious problems, but if you stop breathing for even a short time, things go dark in a hurry. For the most part, we breathe without thinking about it. But most of the time, our breathing is fast. Science and lots of religious traditions agree that something powerful happens when you breathe correctly—deeply. Breathing deeply can actually help calm your mind and body.

In counseling school, we learned that if you breathe correctly, like a baby—with deep breaths from your belly, not short puffs from your chest—your body resists stress. (You'll know you've got it right when your belly puffs out, rather than your chest.) Correct breathing relaxes you.

As we discussed a few chapters ago, when we feel threatened, our body tightens up and goes into fight-or-flight mode. Your muscles tense, your heart beats faster, and your breathing speeds up. You can't control your heart rate, but you can control your breathing.

Most of us take about fifteen breaths per minute. If you can breathe in more slowly, taking about four seconds to inhale, then six seconds to exhale, you'll cut that frantic breathing in half and calm your body down. Your body will naturally respond by relaxing.

Just breathe.

As the pace of the day gets going, it's really easy to forget to breathe deeply. So a great way to start your day is to make sure you breathe correctly—deeply—for a few intentional minutes each day. I do five to ten minutes of deep breathing in the morning. No matter how the morning started, it calms me down physically and mentally. I've found it also helps my morning devotional times be more focused when I start by getting my breathing under control. I highly suggest you try it. Write it on your mirror or a note card so you see it first thing in the morning: BREATHE. Then practice it for a few minutes to start the day. You'll get better at it. The great thing is, you can breathe anywhere. Waiting for your delayed flight. Sitting at the traffic light. Breathing throughout the day can help you get to a place of peace and solitude.

This small step can open the door to a peace that you may have never thought possible. Breathing is a great way to bring yourself into a place of solitude and peace. It's a great way to clear your mind and calm your body. Which is why I believe we need to dedicate an entire day to taking a deep breath.

A Day-Long Breath

I lead a hike through Israel in which we walk in the footsteps of Jesus from Nazareth to the Mount of Beatitudes. We stop in Cana—where Jesus did his first miracle—then head up Mount Arbel, over the Horns of Hattin—the site of a famous Crusader battle—and down to Magdala and Capernaum on the shores of Galilee. During our final night of the hike, we stay at the convent on Mount of Beatitudes.

The first time I did the hike, I had the whole trip scheduled, but when I went to book the accommodations, I ran into a roadblock I hadn't anticipated. One of our overnight stops was scheduled at an Orthodox Jewish kibbutz, a collective farm. Orthodox Jews won't take guests from Friday night to Saturday night because that twenty-four-hour period is their sacred Shabbat, their Sabbath day of rest. They are strict about it. So strict that I had to rearrange our entire schedule around it.

Most of Israel, particularly Jerusalem, completely shuts down on Shabbat. All but a handful of restaurants and stores close. They take it so seriously that most buildings there are equipped with Shabbat elevators. The buttons are disabled so you don't "work" by pushing them. Instead, the elevator stops at each floor, opens, then closes. If you are staying on the thirtieth floor and accidentally end up on one of these elevators … talk about slowing down. Some hotels won't even let you use their coffee makers on Shabbat. (A sure formula for frustration and anger!) That societal pressure there to slow down one day per week makes it a lot easier to take a day of rest seriously. But you probably can't remove button-pushing from your life on a particular day. We tend to get swept up in the full-on, everyday nature of our culture. Which makes it all the more important for us to be intentional and serious about rearranging our schedules to accommodate a day to rest and breathe. I see Sabbath as a day-long breath.

We are made to work and create. Working hard is a good thing. But we're also made to need rest. If you've ever taken on a strict exercise regimen, you know a good trainer will make you take rest days for your muscles to recover. Those recovery days actually make you stronger. When we don't take time to rest, it can have horrible consequences. As productivity increases around the world, we are seeing the harmful effects of too much work. In fact, for a while, Japan experienced an epidemic of people dying from something they called *karōshi*—that is, working to death.[2] When life is all work and no rest, you can be certain that at some point things are going to turn ugly.

In the Genesis story of creation, God spent six days working, and then He rested. The Psalms seem to indicate that God never sleeps, so I doubt He actually slept, but you can be certain it was a time that

God kicked back, took a deep breath, and enjoyed what He had created. We need that time too. We need time to enjoy the fruits of our labor. We need time to relax and process the results of our work.

Making a bunch of strict rules about not working leads to legalism and control, so that's not the goal here. But it is wise to set some parameters for what our day-long breath will look like. A Sabbath day shouldn't be a time to catch up on all the stuff you didn't get done during the week. That defeats the whole purpose! Taking a Sabbath may mean things are left undone. Some laundry may be left unfolded for a day. The home project may not get done this week. Cut yourself some slack. Don't worry. You're resourceful; you'll get that other stuff done eventually. But you'll get it done even faster and better if you are rested when you do it.

You may work on the weekends, so the traditional rest days of Saturday or Sunday may not work for you. But you can choose any day. Just establish a plan beforehand for how you'll give yourself time to just breathe. Do meal preparation the night before. Use a slow cooker to prepare it. Send all calls to voicemail for the day. Don't schedule anything but family time on those days.

Rest looks different for everyone. Sometimes it means actually sleeping. But it can also mean just taking focused time to enjoy life and not worry about work. Richard Foster talks about how "the church Fathers often spoke of Otium Sanctum: 'holy leisure.' It refers to a sense of balance in life, an ability to be at peace through the activities of the day, an ability to rest and take time to enjoy beauty, an ability to pace ourselves."[3] You can be moving and still be at rest. You can rest while kayaking down a river. (Cooking is rest for me. Seriously. It helps me relax and process my life as I create.) You can rest while reading an instructional book. The litmus test is this: Does it rejuvenate you and remind you that you don't need to run the world? Sabbath is an act of faith. It's trusting that God will keep things running while you take a breather. (Of course, He's always keeping things running … maybe we should breathe a lot more easily all of the time.)

Like everything else I've shared so far, you don't need to do *more* to get the benefits. You're already breathing. So why not start to do it intentionally? I'm certain that if you do, you'll start to see results. Breathing correctly opens the door to solitude. Slowly but surely, you'll find yourself more at peace. You'll find yourself more aware of what's happening around you. You'll start to see things beyond the hurry and urgency of your life. Which will naturally lead to the next practice that will bring peace.

Contemplate

*The opposite of contemplation is not
action—it is reaction.*

—*Richard Rohr*

The first time I shared my outdoor adventure idea with my friend
Mark, his face lit up. Turns out he had just developed a little formula that perfectly encapsulates what happens on that kind of adventure trip:

Change of Pace + Change of Place = Change of Perspective

As soon as he said it, I decided I'd adopt that as the motto for what
would become Summit Leaders. There's nothing like getting out of
your normal routine and pace of life to get a whole new perspective
on your life. And honestly, for most of us, we don't need a major life
overhaul; we just need to see things from another point of view.

You may not be able to hike to Machu Picchu or raft the Grand
Canyon, but the good news is you don't have to. There's a spiritual
discipline people have been practicing for centuries that brings a
change of perspective. That spiritual discipline is contemplation.

Love slows down to contemplate.

Hitting Life before It Hits Back

I work with a lot of very driven, Type-A people. I know this whole section of the book is wading into some uncomfortable waters for those folks. I can hear their responses already: "Look, this solitude and breathing and contemplation thing is nice, but I've got real challenges, man. I don't have time for all this passive sitting around. I need action-based solutions."

I get it. For years, the idea of contemplation seemed like a worthless use of time to me. Navel-gazing. I saw it as being for those who didn't have anything better to accomplish. Most of the "contemplative" types I've known are weird. They read into all sorts of random things. "That budding flower is telling me how my destiny will unfold, bro ..."

Yeah ... Not my thing.

Contemplation doesn't come naturally for me. I am a man of action. I tend to jump out of bed and attack the day. Otherwise, I know it will attack me. So rather than have it control me, I do my best to control it.

But here's the problem: If you haven't noticed yet, life is an endless stream of challenges. It never lets up. As hard as you try, you will never get the edge on life's problems. Solve one, and another pops up. There are always more problems. But I've learned from personal experience that contemplation isn't passive. In fact, contemplation is about actively seeking another way of seeing the world around you. Contemplation gives you an edge on the challenges you face by helping you see them from a new perspective.

If you look up contemplation in the dictionary, it will say: "the action of looking thoughtfully at something for a long time." Contemplation *is* action-based. Even the definition says so. Contemplation isn't introspection or self-analysis. That can be a small element of it—it has its place. But contemplation isn't about trying to see things better from your perspective. You already know what you see. Your very real problems have consumed your thoughts for hours, and you still don't have solutions. You need another perspective.

Contemplation is higher-level thinking.

Albert Einstein is credited with having said: "No problem can be solved from the same level of consciousness that created it." The problems we see in the physical world can't be solved in the physical world. They require a deeper level of insight. Which may be why Einstein also said, "I want to know God's thoughts—the rest are mere details." One of the most brilliant minds that ever lived seemed to understand that we don't need more of our own perspective to solve life's challenges. We need a higher one.

The goal is to see things as they really are. The goal is to get God's perspective on life. Contemplation helps us slow down and get in tune with what the Creator says is truth.

In *The Great Divorce*, C.S. Lewis told a fictional story about a guy who got to visit Heaven. When he arrived, he started walking barefoot through a beautiful field of grass. But the grass hurt his feet. Someone explained to the character that Heaven is so real that he can't handle it because he's not yet a "solid one,"[1] someone who is completely in touch with the reality of what is. I believe that contemplation has a way of getting us in touch with a higher reality. Contemplation helps us see things as they really are. It makes us solid, so we can face what's real. It reveals the real issues and the real solutions. Contemplation helps us look past the chaos, noise, and urgency. We look a little deeper to get a bigger perspective on what is true.

When we live angry and in crisis mode, we lose perspective. There's always some pain calling for attention. If it's not already hurting, we're afraid it might start to. Like I said before, fear-based living causes you to home in on avoiding the one thing you fear the most. It shrinks your world. We stop thinking about the future or God's faithfulness in the past and get laser-focused on what's yelling loudest. What's loudest usually is our anxiety about not getting security, connection, and control. We end up losing perspective on anything beyond how our immediate needs can be met and how we can meet them ourselves. We really want to believe God is at work in our lives, but all the evidence around us seems to indicate otherwise. So we speed up and go faster. But when we slow down, take time for solitude, and practice contemplation, it opens the door for the expert—our Creator—to give us insight into our lives. It helps us begin to see the world through His eyes. And that changes everything.

Next-Level Insights

There isn't much I wouldn't do for my daughter if she asked me. Even if I'm busy, when she comes asking me to play with her, if at all possible, I drop everything to give her my time (especially if she's playing with Legos). I love giving her what she asks for. But what really gets my heart fluttering is when she asks me to explain something to her, and she really listens. I love seeing her brain begin to understand something new in a clear way.

God loves it when we ask Him for things. Our requests are always welcome. He'll always be there. But asking for help is entry-level prayer. Next-level prayer starts when we get quiet and start to listen for His direction. He made us. He knows exactly what we need. Really. I've found that a lot of the time, I don't really know what to ask for. I *think* I do. I ask, "God, make my child behave. God take away my anger." We pray for the symptoms, but God wants to heal the real, deeper problem. As my friend James Fields says, "God always heals, but He doesn't always heal the part of us that hurts. He faithfully heals the part of us that hinders love...."[2]

Contemplative prayer is about listening for His insight.

Solitude and insight tend to go hand in glove. Creative researchers talk about something called the Three Bs: the bathtub, the bed, and the bus. There are loads of stories of how people have their greatest epiphanies in showers, when they wake up with a brilliant idea, or on public transport. When our mind gets a break from directly thinking about a problem and we change our pace, our mental energy shifts to another part of the brain. The solution appears from a different area of our gray matter. A famous example of this is a NASA engineer who was trying to figure out how to fix a major distortion problem with the lenses of the Hubble Space Telescope. He came up with the solution while showering in a European hotel that was based on the way the showerhead was constructed.[3] Change of pace and place.

One researcher explained the phenomenon this way:

> When our minds are at ease—when those alpha waves are rippling through the brain—we're more likely to direct the spotlight of attention inward, toward that stream of remote associations emanating from the right hemisphere. In contrast, when we are diligently focused, our attention tends to be directed outward, toward the details of the problems we're trying to solve. While this pattern of attention is necessary when solving problems analytically, it actually prevents us from detecting the connections that lead to insights.[4]

I believe all good ideas come from God, so I tend to attribute those epiphanies to His giving insight when we stop trying to figure out the problem on our own. My dad calls this process "turning it over to your spirit." If you have a relationship with Christ, the Spirit of God is actually living in you. Stop focusing on the problem and focus on connection with His Spirit that is alive in you. Sure, think hard about the problem. But when you can't find the solution, turn it over to your spirit. It's a counterintuitive way to approach a problem, but God wants to give you the insight you need if you'll look to Him for the solution.

While I was writing this book, I got stuck on the third section about creating space. Something wasn't right, but I couldn't figure out what it was. I moved so many paragraphs around so many times over multiple days that I started to question the logic of everything I had written. I realized my brain was fried and that I needed to pray for insight. I decided to practice this very thing—turning it over to my spirit. So I prayed. Then I stopped thinking about it. When my mind wanted to start ruminating on it again, I forced myself to stop. Two days later, I popped awake at 4:00 a.m. and knew exactly what I needed to do to fix the chapter. It was in front of me the whole time, but I just couldn't see it.

Stop worrying, stressing, and driving yourself crazy trying to figure out the solution to your problem. Let God make the connection between your challenge and His solution. When we give space in our minds for God's thoughts to enter, He will provide answers.

How to Contemplate

Contemplation is an odd activity because it's not about doing something. It's about not doing something. Henri Nouwen says it best:

> Contemplative prayer is not a way of being busy with God instead of with people, but it is an attitude in which we recognize God's ultimate priority by being useless in his presence.... It cuts a hole in our busyness and reminds us and others that it is God and not we who creates and sustains the world.[5]

Just like making space for our priorities, contemplative prayer is about making space for God to give us insight. It's slowing down long enough for Him to speak in His whisper. The challenge with this kind of prayer is that there's no formula for it. Based on personal experience, you will have days, weeks, or sometimes months where you will practice this kind of prayer and walk away feeling like you have no more insight than when you started. You have to trust that God is still working, but it may be slower than you want. Something Pierre Teilhard de Chardin said always helps me remember to be patient with how God is working and revealing His truth through contemplation in our lives:

> Above all, trust in the slow work of God.
> We are quite naturally impatient in everything to reach the end without delay.
> We should like to skip the intermediate stages.
> We are impatient of being on the way to something unknown, something new.
> And yet it is the law of all progress that it is made by passing through some stages of instability—and that it may take a very long time.
> And so I think it is with you; your ideas mature gradually—let them grow, let them shape themselves, without undue haste.
> Don't try to force them on, as though you could be today what time (that is to say, grace and circumstances acting on your own good will) will make of you tomorrow.
> Only God could say what this new spirit gradually forming within you will be.
> Give Our Lord the benefit of believing that his hand is leading you, and accept the anxiety of feeling yourself in suspense and incomplete.[6]

It may take longer than you want for the answers to appear. And some may never be clear on this side of eternity. But they will appear.

You can trust that God is working, and in contemplative prayer we can get a glimpse of His work—if we'll slow down and take the time to listen.

Thousands of books have been written about contemplative prayer. There's always more to learn about it. I encourage you to read books by Henri Nouwen, Richard Foster, and Dallas Willard. They have some great insights on contemplative prayer. But my simple goal in this chapter is to help you see that slowing down to spend time listening to God is a major key to calming fear, releasing anger, and making sure hurry doesn't consume you. It's a tried-and-true practice, and you will always get results from it. Contemplation leads to next-level insight.

20

Meditate

*All of humanity's problems stem from man's inability to
sit quietly in a room.*

—*Blaise Pascal*

A few years back, I took a team on a safari to the Ngorongoro Crater, a giant game reserve in the middle of Tanzania that has one of the highest concentrations of African wildlife. At one of our stops, while I was looking out a window, a fly bit me. I brushed it away. At that exact moment, our Land Cruiser pulled up next to a green sheet stretched from a tree to the ground.

"What's that green sheet for?" I asked our driver, surveying the red bump on my arm.

"It's to kill tsetse flies."

My stomach tightened. "Tsetse flies?"

"Yes, they kill lots of people around here."

I didn't bother to ask the rationale for parking next to this green sheet that attracted the fly of death. No, I was already freaking out.

I looked at my arm. *I'm a dead man.* I turned to a doctor who was with us. "A fly just bit me. Should I be worried?"

"Probably," he said, smiling.

I knew he was joking, but I was really freaking out now. Catastrophizing. I was about to die. I thought about Emily. *Will I ever see her again?*

When we got to the safari lodge, I quickly googled "tsetse flies." Bad idea! I discovered they give you African sleeping sickness. There is no cure. Sometimes it flares up years after the bite. A *mzungu* (white boy) like me died just a year earlier when he was bitten by a tsetse fly in the exact location I had been that day. For the next several days, my mind was filled with so much worry that I could barely enjoy the rest of the safari.

A good amount of time has passed since that incident, so I think I'm out of the woods and should survive. But this experience was a great reminder of how worry can ruin even the most amazing experiences. Worry can consume you. Just like that bug bite caused my mind to run out of control with all sorts of horrible possibilities, most of us can take the smallest things in our life—a confrontation, election results, a random comment—and turn them into the end of the world in our minds.

Our powerful minds are a gift. But if they're always thinking about the negative and terrible possibilities, they can feel like a curse. Focusing on the negative can lead us to some really bad thought patterns.

We talked about ruminating in the chapter on forgiveness. Ruminating is chewing on the same thing over and over. Like a cow that chews its cud. It's kind of disgusting to think about, but that's a pretty good picture of what happens when we worry—we chew on negative thoughts over and over.

But here's the good news: if you can worry, you can turn that around into its positive form—meditation.

Believe it or not, you and I already meditate a lot. We just meditate on the wrong stuff. You meditated at 2:30 a.m. when you were up rehearsing that awkward conversation you have to have at work. You meditated all day on that biopsy the doctor sent off to get checked. You meditated on the horrible thing your ex said to you when he ended the relationship. When you focus on what's negative and worry about what could go wrong, you are meditating. It's just meditation on bad things. Meditation and worrying involve the same mental process.

Worrying is ruminating on all the negative.

Meditation is ruminating on the positive.

When we slow down, keep our thoughts from running wild, and meditate on the right things, we focus on what is good and right and true in the world rather than the tyranny of fear and anxiety that is screaming for our attention.

Love slows down to meditate.

Checking In with Your Thoughts

In college, I had a job that involved some shifts with crazy hours. One month, my shift at work got adjusted, and I started sharing a fifteen-minute break with a lady who was particularly negative. During the entire break, she would talk about all the things wrong in the world. Bosses, injustice, the weather. Trying to relate to her, I started sharing things that annoyed me. We'd go back and forth while complaining for the entire break. Before long, I really started to dislike my job. I started seeing all the problems at my company. A few months later, I got transferred back to my regular shift. One day, I was sitting with a friend over lunch break, and right in the middle of our conversation, she got up, took her lunch, and walked out. I asked her where she was going. She said, "I can't be around you. You're so negative." I hadn't even realized just how much my thoughts and perspective had gotten out of control. I was always thinking and talking about the negative. So all I saw was negative.

Our minds are powerful. So we have to pay close attention to what we're using that mental power to do. I know for me, worry and anxiety can sneak into my thoughts so quickly and subtly that I don't even realize I'm digging a huge hole of negativity. We all tend to use our minds to focus on very specific things—and usually, those tend to be negative, without even realizing the pattern. That's why I have a little notecard in my office that says:

"Think about what you are thinking about."

That's part of what Peter was talking about when he said to "be alert and of sober mind. Your enemy the devil prowls around like a roaring lion looking for someone to devour."[1] Your mind is going to focus on something. If you aren't alert, your thoughts can devour you with negativity. But that same power of thought can be used to think about what's true and right. So why not choose to focus on all the good?

Meditation chooses to focus on what is good and true and right. It keeps what's positive at the forefront of our thoughts and actually has a way of transforming how we see the world. Sure, there are all sorts of negative and horrible things happening around us. But there's also lots of good. We get to decide what we focus on.

King David said that the person who meditates on truth day and night "is like a tree planted by streams of water, which yields its fruit in season, and whose leaf does not wither—whatever they do prospers."[2] Like a tree by the water—strong and unshaken. Can you imagine what that could look like? Rather than being worried about all the bad around you, you'd have a quiet confidence. The waters may rise, but the floods of worry and anxiety won't uproot you. The storms may blow, but your roots are deep, and you aren't going anywhere.

That's the power of meditating on truth. It makes you really, really strong.

So on what, pray tell, should we meditate? Great question. Here are a few great things to start meditating on.

Scripture

There's a reason Christians are so obsessed with the Bible. We're convinced it is actually God's revelation of what is real and what works. The Bible tells tales of cold reality. Murder. Jealousy. Fear. It's real. But there's also a thread of hope that weaves the whole story together. That hope is Jesus. The whole Bible points to Jesus and redemption. That's our hope in this world.

We've already established that if you want life to go well, value what Jesus values. He's the center of what is real. His life is *the* example—the way He responded to people, the authority He walked in. Jesus was fearless. He even showed us how to use anger properly. He is the ideal. He is the ultimate reality. When we meditate on His life and the stories leading up to His epic act of saving the world, we get a glimpse of what's real. It shows us how we can live in touch with reality.

Fill your mind with God's thoughts. Just read the Bible, even if you don't understand it all. Then ask God to show you what it means. Turn it over to your spirit through contemplation. The Apostle James said, "If any of you lacks wisdom, let him ask God, who gives generously to all without reproach, and it will be given him."[3] God can give you wisdom about His word. Once you think you've got clarity on a particular part of Scripture, run it past a few wise folks and make sure it's in line with the rest of the Bible. If you can, memorize small verses that you find encouraging. Write them on notecards and place them where you can easily see them. Let them remind you of truth throughout the day. Fill your mind with God's thoughts from Scripture.

Nature

I joked about people who say flowers speak to them. But the thing is, they actually can speak about God. In fact, Jesus used loads of examples from nature. He said to look at the flowers and the birds and mountains for examples of how to not worry and how to have faith. The whole world points to God.

Nature is not God, but it always points to God. I can't tell you how many times I've gotten insight on my life while hiking outdoors. But you have to really pay attention to what's happening around you. Lots of people get focused on the destination when they're hiking rather than the journey. They miss the message of God all around them. This doesn't just happen in hiking, by the way. It happens in life, but I digress.

You may not be an avid outdoor person. That's fine. But don't miss out on meditating on God in nature. Find an environment that fits you. It may be the ocean or a muddy river in your town. It may be a small park in the middle of a busy city. Maybe it's watching your dog. (But not your cat—cats are the devil.) Just breathe and observe. Think about God's power revealed in nature. God gives us glimpses of who He is through every piece of nature—even cats.

Seasons of Life

Life happens in seasons. There are happy, spring seasons of new life. There are winter seasons where it seems everything we love is dying off. Sometimes we don't realize the value of a season because we're so anxious to get to the next season, or because the whole season feels like we're losing everything we know. But never forget this: Every season has a purpose. You just may not see it right now. Meditate on God's faithfulness in every season.

Søren Kierkegaard said, "Life is lived forward. But it can only be understood looking backward." That's the value of spending time meditating on God's work in our lives. It gives us perspective on how far He has brought us. Frederick Buechner talks about the power of meditating on your life when he says:

Listen to your life. See it for the fathomless mystery it is. In the boredom and pain of it, no less than in the excitement and gladness: touch, taste, smell your way to the holy and hidden heart of it, because in the last analysis all moments are key moments, and life itself is grace.[4]

God is always at work in your life. There are some experiences in life we won't understand on this side of eternity, but God wants to use everything that has happened to you—good, bad, and ugly—to prepare you for what is next. He wants to use your history to lead you to your calling. Meditate on the good God has brought into your life. He has been faithful in the past, and He will be faithful in the future.

It's a Matter of Focus

A guy who was in the military joined my coaching program a few years ago. During a deployment to the Middle East, he had some pretty traumatic experiences. He struggled to sleep for the next several years. He tried doctors, counselors, and pills to get relief. Nothing worked. Eventually, he just resigned himself to the fact that he'd probably always struggle with sleep.

I didn't know he had this problem, but we talked about meditation in one part of the program. He started meditating on Bible passages in the morning and found that it calmed his mind for the day. So he decided to meditate on Scripture right before bed rather than watch TV or read.

Then something incredible happened.

For the first time in years, he was able to sleep through the night. Meditation did what doctors, counselors, and pills couldn't! When he called to tell me this amazing news, it immediately reminded me of Isaiah 26:3: "You keep him in perfect peace whose mind is stayed on you, because he trusts in you." Meditation helped him through anxiety and post-traumatic stress. When you put truth into your mind, it will set you free. When your mind is focused on what is good and true and right, it brings peace, confidence, and joy, instead of hurry, worry, and anger.

Meditation starts with making sure you're focused on whatever is "true, whatever is honorable, whatever is just, whatever is pure, whatever is lovely, whatever is commendable; if there is any excellence, if there is anything worthy of praise, think about these things."[5] Fill your mind with truth about God. Repeat it over and over until that truth becomes part of who you are and what you believe. The goal isn't to ignore the bad things out there. The goal is to make sure that we don't let those negative things shift our perspective in a way that causes us to miss out on the overwhelming amount of truth and goodness in our world.

Meditation 101

Just like all the other practices we've talked about in this section, you don't have to go to a remote cabin in the Rockies or check yourself into a retreat center to get started meditating. You don't have to do more. You just need to make an adjustment. It's not that complicated. You can start meditating right here and now. Meditation takes place on the foundation of the breathing and contemplation we already talked about. Start by thinking about what you are thinking about. Is it mostly negative? Then get intentional about getting your mind focused on good things, rather than anxiety and worry. If your mind starts slipping into negativity, don't get all down on yourself. Just start thinking about all the good around you. Look for where you see love, joy, peace, patience, and kindness all around you. Focus on those things.

Find a simple truth and start focusing on it. Take the verse I mentioned earlier, Isaiah 26:3: "You keep him in perfect peace whose mind is stayed on you, because he trusts in you."

Write it on a little notecard. It should be pretty easy to memorize it too. When you feel anger or worry in your mind, catch yourself and start repeating that verse. Replace the negative thought pattern with a positive thought pattern. Chew on it. Repeat it.

You don't have to live in constant worry and anxiety. You can get peace and joy right in the middle of even the hardest circumstances when you choose to meditate on what is true and good. Shift your worry into meditation, and you'll find a new sense of confidence coming from deep within you. When you walk with that kind of hope and joy, you become a source of life to those around you. Which leads to the next value that is of highest importance—people.

PART VI

Walk with Others

21

Walk with Others

If you want to go fast, go alone.
If you want to go far, go with others.

—*African Proverb*

I'm a slow hiker. I used to try to keep my hiking teams all walking together, but I learned early on that people hike at different paces. Trying to keep the entire team walking in step just isn't possible. The teams naturally break into three or four groups, hiking at similar paces throughout the day. There's usually a group of really in-shape folks who end up getting to our destination way before everyone else.

On one particular trip to Machu Picchu, one of those super-strong hikers was Michele. She's a fun-loving, full-of-life doctor who has summited some of the highest peaks in America. She and her husband, Jon, also climbed Kilimanjaro with me. She's strong. I never bother to try to keep pace with her because she'll beat me every time.

On the final stretch of our hike to Machu Picchu, she and our guide Elias bolted ahead, determined to beat everyone else to Inti Punku, the Sun Gate, where we would enter the ancient ruins. Michele told me they were the first hikers in our group to the gate by a long stretch. Elias glanced at his watch, raised his eyebrows, and proclaimed, "Forty-two minutes! Pretty good!"

Michele calculated that they had just completed three miles (five kilometers) uphill, at elevation, with a backpack, in forty-two minutes. For obvious reasons, she was feeling pretty confident. (For the record, that really is impressive; I've never done it in less than two hours!) Out of curiosity, she asked our guide, "What's your fastest time for this segment?"

He smiled. "Twenty-one minutes!"

Half the time.

Michele said she felt pretty humbled. "He was showing a lot of meekness."

I think her description of our guide pretty much nailed it.

Meekness isn't weakness. Meekness is strength under control. It's choosing to slow down, even though we could go faster, to walk with others on the journey.

We all move through life at a unique pace. It's OK to move at your own pace. It's OK to pursue personal dreams and goals. But if you're going your own pace and start to realize that you feel alone, or really are all alone, there's a good chance you need to slow down and find someone to walk with. It shouldn't be lonely at the top. We aren't meant to walk through life alone.

Love slows down to walk with others.

People Slow You Down

I mentioned a few chapters back that the first time I climbed Mount Kilimanjaro I didn't make it to the top. I was in the best shape of my life. I was laser-focused on getting to the top. But I felt like I was in competition with my team members. I had to prove myself. I was so goal-focused that I never spent time building relationships with others on the team. That trip did not go well.

The next time I attempted Kili, I went with a lot more humility. I brought a team. That team included Bob Goff, one of the most encouraging people I've ever met. Bob set the tone. The entire hike, the team was speaking life and encouragement over each other. I wasn't in nearly as good of shape as the first time I climbed it, and I was about twelve years older, but our entire team made it to the top this time. I attribute that to the strength we had as a team. You will always go further and climb higher when you have a strong, encouraging team around you. And you'll all make it to the top.

If it feels lonely at the top, you may be going too fast. If no one is there to enjoy success with you, or if they just don't like being around you and your franticness, it's a clear sign that your pace is a problem. It's easy to get so focused on a goal that, unintentionally, we end up leaving our families, employees, or kids behind in a cloud of dust. But meekness chooses to regulate our pace so we make sure we are always doing the journey with others in community.

Jesus said the meek will inherit the earth.[1] We've all had that one teacher who modeled meekness. That teacher was willing to spend some extra time helping us. All the other teachers just said, "Read the book and you'll learn it." But that one teacher took the time to slow down and really teach you. We never forget that teacher. She or he goes with us throughout our lives. I think that's part of the inheritance Jesus was talking about. When we slow down and use our strength to help others, we extend ourselves beyond just ourselves—a part of us lives on in others. But healthy relationships aren't just one-sided. We get strength and fulfillment from the relationships too. We succeed when we help others succeed.

We live in a fast-paced world. We're all climbing the mountain that we think will bring us the security, connection, and control we want. We're trying to get ahead, or at least to keep up with the rat race. We're constantly comparing ourselves with others, trying to figure out if we're ahead or behind. We evaluate our lives based on the people around us. The problem is, those same people are comparing themselves to us. They feel just as behind as you and I do. Most of us feel like we don't have enough hours in the day to accomplish our dreams. We're fighting to keep up and—ideally—get ahead. That drive can be helpful when it's in balance. But a clear sign that your ambition is out of balance is when people begin to feel like a burden or your competition.

If you've been in a relationship where you got hurt or the other person left you, then it's tempting to think people just aren't worth the effort. People create all sorts of drama and issues. (In fact, if you know a group of people who don't have issues, then *you* are probably their issue!) We've all got shortcomings and flaws. We're grouchy and insecure and incompetent, and sometimes just downright nasty. But people are what God values most. So if we want to seek God's Kingdom and His values first to ensure everything else falls into line, relationships need to be of highest value.

The most tangible expressions of giving and receiving love are felt through other people. Your achieving your hopes and dreams will always be connected to your helping others achieve their hopes and dreams. Walking with others in community is the key to achieving your destiny.

That Lonely Feeling

When Emily and I moved to Peru, we went to start a church with another couple who were going to start a café as part of the ministry. Within just a few months of moving, the other couple had to return to the United States, and we found ourselves taking over the task of starting the café as well. I didn't know what I was doing, so I started asking the different missionaries who lived in our community for their help with it. They were all busy with their own ministries, but I asked anyway.

The first guy I asked said, "I've been wondering when someone would ask. I was a four-star chef in London before we moved here.

I'm happy to help." Another guy told me, "Sure, I used to design cafés in London before I moved here." (Thank heavens for Londoners!) We got that café open faster than I ever could've imagined. The former chef helped us design a menu. He hired and trained our staff. He helped us understand how to make money in the food business. All the help we needed to thrive was already around us; we just had to reach out.

Let me be blunt about this: You can't make it in this world alone. You just can't. You are not a rock or an island. "Pull yourself up by your bootstraps!" isn't Jesus. It's Texas. Which is where I live, so I have to constantly fight the pride inside me that says I can go it alone. It's humbling to admit that I need others. I can tell I'm trying to carry the load alone when I start getting angry and frustrated. I'm most vulnerable to discouragement and depression when I'm trying to walk alone and do it on my own.

The Apostle Peter warned us to pay close attention to our thoughts because we have an enemy who is like a roaring lion. Lions roar as an intimidation tactic to get a herd of animals nervous and on the run. As soon as one animal separates from the herd, they get singled out for attack. The same thing happens when we start running away from community.

For years, I've seen a pattern of running from community that always concerns me. Faithful members of the church will disappear for weeks. We'll call to check on them, and they have all sorts of reasons for being gone: kids' sports, family vacation, work. Sometimes those folks reappear after a few weeks and act like they've never been gone. Other times we'll hear that they're divorcing their spouses.

I finally got up the nerve to ask one guy who had disappeared for a while what had really happened. He said, "My wife and I were having some marriage problems and we didn't want anyone to know, so we pulled away until we could work it out." That guy and his wife eventually got divorced. I was sad to hear it, but it didn't surprise me.

They fell for the classic mistake of pulling away and separating themselves from the community that could actually give them strength.
When you feel stressed, being around others is often the last thing you
want to do. Pulling away seems easier. But the fact is that pushing into
community when you feel overwhelmed is actually the best thing you
can do.

A researcher named Shawn Achor spent years studying what leads
to happiness. He discovered that the key predictor of success when
people are under stress is their social engagement.[2] When people were
under major stress, the more time they spent with others, the better
they shouldered the challenges in their lives. But that's the opposite of
what most of us do. When things get hard, most of us pull away, trying
to figure out how to handle it on our own. Sometimes it's out of pride,
not wanting to show weakness. Other times we just don't want to
burden others with our struggles. But when we isolate ourselves, we
pull away from the very thing that can strengthen us. It leaves us out
in the cold. A coal that gets separated from the fire will always lose
heat in a hurry. Stay warm and stay close to community.

You are not alone unless you choose to be.

There are people around you who understand and can walk with
you through whatever you're facing—wayward kids, anxiety, addictions. They may not be facing the exact situation you are, but that
doesn't mean they can't help you walk through it. Don't believe the lie
that you're alone. Don't believe the lie that no one understands your
pain. There are people all around you who can walk with you through
whatever you are facing. You just have to be willing to reach out. Make
community and time with others a priority.

The Inefficient Life

Our mailbox is about two blocks from our house. When my
daughter sees me grab the key from the hook by the door, she knows

I'm going to get the mail. She always wants to join me for the walk, which typically turns a two-minute process into a ten-minute ordeal. Sometimes I slip out while she isn't watching so I don't have to bring her along. But lately, I've been rethinking that. There is something powerful happening on those walks. She feels part of what I'm doing; she feels valued. I don't need her help, but she feels validated when I bring her in on the process.

Slowing down to walk with others isn't necessarily efficient. In fact, making time for community is often inconvenient. It's a lot of work and energy to be part of a small group during the school year or serve at a church or community group. It may bring drama into your life that you don't think you have time for. Leaving space on the weekend for nothing but quality time with people, just hanging out, can seem like a waste. You may have to sacrifice some good things in your life to make sure you have time and energy to invest in spending time with others. But trust me on this: building community is never a waste of time or energy.

I'm convinced that when you decide to take community seriously, you'll see that God has already placed a great group of people around you. The community you need is available around you. You may have to lead the charge in bringing the people together. Other people are busy too, so you may need to develop a plan for how you can make time to be with those around you. It'll take some work. But I guarantee it'll be worth it.

Just keep something in mind: Having people around you isn't enough. It's possible to be in a crowd and still feel alone. So once you find that community, there are a few decisions you'll need to make to slow down and get the most from it. Which is what we'll talk about next.

22

Be Present

Future love does not exist.
Love is a present activity only.
The man who does not manifest love
in the present has not love.

—Leo Tolstoy

At the beginning of every trip I lead, I have an orientation with the team members. I encourage them to check in with their families before doing their best to disconnect from life back home. Put away the phone, stop checking social media, ignore the emails. I've seen way too many people miss out on the fullness of the experience because they stayed too connected to what they left behind.

Usually by the second day of the hike, all the team members are fully engaged and present. But for those who are still connected, eventually we get to a place where they lose that last bar of cell service. They sigh, turn off their phones, and put them in their backpacks. That's when the good stuff starts happening. It's amazing to see just how quickly people bond with total strangers when they change their pace and place together. They get to know each other and their stories very quickly. They become a real team, encouraging and supporting each other on the trip.

But something happens on the last night of the journey. They realize the "real" world is about to hit them in the face again. They took a sneak peek at their inbox or voicemails when we got service, and they know it's going to be overwhelming when they get back home. By the time we do our final team meeting, it's hard to keep them engaged and present.

You know who's the worst about staying engaged? Me. The instant I get mobile phone service (at this point on most hikes, I know the exact spot between the mountains where I get it), I call and check in with Emily. At that moment, my mind is off what's happening right now and on to the worries of something happening far away that I can't currently do anything about. I check out.

I don't have to be on a mountain in Africa or deep in the Andes for this to happen. It happens nearly every evening in my own home. I'll pick up my phone to check what time it is and see that an email arrived. I open it. It needs my attention. I don't want it to wait until tomorrow, even though it's 7:00 p.m. So I check back into work and check out of home life. Thanks to technology, there is always something available to draw us out of our world and into another.

And my family notices.

My daughter, Elise, has started doing this new thing where she asks, "Are you back now?" when I've been looking at my phone in her presence. It's kind of convicting. I really try to be present when I'm with her, but for some reason, the allure of people I barely know on social media or flash sales in my email draw my attention away. I can't really engage in loving those around me—giving them my best—when I am not truly present.

Love slows down to be present.

The Fear of Missing Out

I took a group to Paris, France, and we stood at a place called Trocadéro, where a large crowd gathers every night to watch the Eiffel Tower light show. At one point, I looked around me and noticed every single person was watching the experience through the filter of a phone or tablet screen. They were there, but not really.

It's hard to fully enjoy a moment when we're focused on trying to capture it. I completely understand wanting to share a moment with others who aren't there. But you and I both know that when we try to share an epic moment in a picture, we always end up saying something like, "Pictures don't do it justice. You had to have been there." And that's the thing: You have to *be there*. Really.

Our world offers so many distractions that being present can take some serious discipline. One group of researchers asked people to share how present and mentally engaged they were with what they were doing at random times during the day. People admitted to being distracted 46.9 percent of the time.[1] Makes me wonder if most of us are missing out on about half our lives because we're distracted.

We have access to the entire world on our phones. When the whole world is at your fingertips, there's always something faster, shinier, or happier going on that we can search for. As soon as our little world gets boring or uncomfortable, we can check into the digital world. And the digital world always has something more interesting than what's happening in front of us.

Enter FOMO. Fear of Missing Out.

We're constantly scanning TV channels or scrolling through social media to see what else is happening. To really start engaging with others, we have to become content with missing out. As soon as you commit to focusing on one thing, you will always miss out on something else—and that's OK. Look at it as a sacrifice. And the right sacrifice always brings meaning to our choices. When you know there is probably something more exciting out there, but you choose to give that up to give your best to what is in front of you, you've made a choice to invest yourself in this present moment. Being present is an act of real love in our world of limitless distractions.

There's one simple discipline that I believe is the most tangible way to show presence in this loud world. That discipline is really listening.

The Best Kind of Presence

A few years back, I set a goal to read at least one hundred books per year. My problem is that I am a slow reader. Someone recommended that I start listening to audiobooks. I did and got hooked! The best part is that by using my phone app, I can speed up the reading to double or triple speed. Sometimes I get through a ten-hour read in three hours. It makes me feel like I'm winning at life.

I know this will sound horrible, so don't judge me. But sometimes I wish I could speed up some of the conversations I have every day. I could get a lot more done. Humans can understand about 400 words per minute. But most people only talk at 125 words per minute. Listening to people is an incredibly inefficient process. But in this loud and distracted world, compassionate listening is the simplest and most powerful gift you can give people. You can't always fix another person's problems, but you can always listen.

Real listening is hard. You can't listen in a hurry. It takes a lot of focus, and you have to really think about what the person is saying. Rather than really listening, our brains oftentimes are buzzing, trying to think of the next thing we'll say so there won't be any awkward pauses. We don't like awkward pauses. But I've found that people don't mind an awkward pause if they're convinced you are really listening.

We all know when someone isn't completely listening. It makes us angry and frustrated. We can read the nonverbal cues. Most of us can even tell when someone isn't present in a phone conversation—checking email, reading something. We know when there is a split-second delay in a person's response. Listening takes lots of discipline. Sometimes we have to jolt ourselves back into focus. To stay focused, you may need to keep eye contact. Move your toes. Relax your shoulders. Change your body position to get comfortable. Making moves like that can show others you really are with them and don't plan on going anywhere soon. There's also nothing wrong with admitting you got mentally distracted and asking the person to repeat what they said. Do whatever it takes to really listen.

When you're able to repeat back—clearly and accurately—what the person said, you've given them a powerful sign that you love them. You've given them your focus and time. It's amazing what you can learn when you really listen. People will tell you pretty much everything about themselves if you'll just listen. But the really important things they have to say may not come out on a set time schedule. Listening isn't convenient, but it can be a big part of what love in action looks like.

What We Miss in a Hurry

I officiated a wedding recently, and at the reception, a man came up to me and said, "I really liked what you said about love." He took a swig of his drink. "It's really frustrating when you're doing all you can to show love and then they go try to commit suicide."

He caught me totally off guard, and I wasn't sure how to respond. "Do you know someone who tried to commit suicide?"

"Yeah. My daughter. I work so hard to give her everything I never got growing up. And then you get a call from your kid's school saying she tried to take her life. Doesn't make sense."

I wasn't sure what to say. "I'm so sorry. Did you see any warning signs beforehand?"

"No. Nothing. I mean, I work lots of hours and pick up overtime on my day off trying to provide for the family. I come home tired." He paused, looking off into the distance for a moment. "It's the bullies. The bullies drove her to this. She was being bullied."

This conversation really jolted me. Someone's deciding to take his or her own life is tragic and involves all sorts of complex factors, including mental illness. I'm not making a statement about suicide here, but what struck me was that the father claimed he never saw it coming.

It was clear that this man loved his family. He was doing the best he could to provide for them. But while he was working away, someone he loved most was struggling—right under his own roof—and he missed it.

We miss things when we aren't present.

But when we are present, it leaves space for us to observe and listen. When people know we are really with them, they're able to express the deeper parts of themselves that can't just be shared on demand.

When I come home from a trip, my wife always wants details. So I share information about what we did, which isn't what she really wants to know. But eventually, after a few days, I'm able to remember conversations and interactions with people—the kind of information she really wants. Relational information. The problem is, I can't just remember all the interactions I had in a snap. It takes me a few days to process and remember. It's like what I talked about in the chapter on creating space: Facts can be produced on demand, but interpretations of those facts take time to emerge. The reason it takes time for relational information to process is a function of how our brains work.

Brain scans have shown that our minds shift into something called the "default mode network" when we're relaxed and not focused on a specific task.[2] The default network focuses on social and relational thoughts—your internal world. Your mind starts thinking about the relational components of your life. That's when the information about what's really driving us, the deeper stuff, comes to the surface. That's why sometimes we don't realize how angry a comment or situation made us until we're driving home from an event. When our minds shift from the external stimuli around us, they start to process the emotions. When we leave room to be present and listen, those around us will have the time they need to share the deeper parts of what is happening in their lives—and that's when we can really love them with compassion.

Compassionate presence always requires an investment of time.

Some researchers got a bunch of seminary students together to test a theory about helping people and being in a hurry. The students were asked to prepare a talk about the Good Samaritan. They were then sent across the campus to another building to give the talk. They were all given different time pressures to get to their talk. Some were told they were already late, so they needed to hurry. Others weren't put under any time pressure.

The researchers positioned an actor who was slumped over and clearly in pain right in the path of the seminary students who were on their way to give a talk about the Good Samaritan. How they responded is pretty telling. "Overall 40% offered some help to the victim. In low-hurry situations, 63% helped, medium-hurry 45% and high-hurry 10%." These pastors-to-be were on their way to talk about the Good Samaritan, a man who helped a hurting person, but when they were in a big rush, only one in ten of the participants actually stopped to *be* a Good Samaritan! Nearly all the participants were concerned by what they had seen when they passed the man, but "they were in a conflict between helping the victim and meeting the needs of the experimenter. Conflict rather than callousness can explain the failure to stop."[3]

Here's my translation: They had two different pressures (dare I say values?) going on at the same time. They saw the hurt person, but being in a hurry didn't allow them to be present for that person. If we are truly going to be present, it can't happen in a hurry. To really show love, we need to make listening and being present priorities. And unless you make them your priorities, people will just seem like a burden, and that will make you frustrated and angry.

Being present won't just happen. You'll have to be intentional. You may even have to give up some good things to leave space for better things. It may require "no-screen" hours at home. After a certain time every evening, no screens—TV, phone, tablet. (Interestingly, studies have shown that looking at bright screens before bed can make it harder to sleep. This presence thing could improve your sleep too!) Leave some space for conversation to emerge. It's much easier to watch shiny screens, but do the hard thing. Just sit around and talk. Play some board games. Be present with those you love for a few hours every night. You might just find your love for them growing!

If you really want to be radical, try a day without any technology. Do your best to limit distractions. If you want to sound super spiritual, call it a technology fast.

Make eye contact. Even if they look away or seem to feel uncomfortable with it, you can be certain that others in your life will walk away from the time with you knowing you were present with them.

Don't google any trivia that arises during a conversation—like who was in that one movie or that politician's age. Get comfortable with not knowing so you can stay present in the conversation. Get comfortable with not needing to correct the details of someone's story. Being present in relationships is usually more important that being right.

You'll notice the difference. You'll feel more connected. You'll feel more love. And the people around you will too.

As you slow down to be present with others, you'll find out what's really going on in their world. And there's a good chance they'll want to know what's really going on in yours.

Be Vulnerable

Vulnerability sounds like truth and feels like courage.
Truth and courage aren't always comfortable,
but they're never weakness.

—Brené Brown

When I first started Summit Leaders, what drew many people to the trip was the big-name speakers I would invite. We got some really influential pastors and authors to hike with us and share their wisdom along the trail. People always walked away from the trips with amazing testimonies and stories about the experience. I was curious about how we could make the experiences even better, so after each trip, I started sending out surveys about what impacted people most. What I learned blew my mind.

Ninety-nine percent of the responses said nothing about the amazing teaching we got from those incredible speakers. What people always mentioned as a life-changing moment on the trip was a conversation they had with another team member. This was baffling to me. We had some of the most insightful, influential Christian leaders in America speaking to these folks, but what made the impact was a normal conversation with another hiker. I followed up on some of the responses and regularly heard team members say things like, "I feel like I got to know people on this team better than people at my church that I've known for years."

After doing this for over ten years, I've learned that when people are outside their normal comfort zones and change their pace and place, they tend to open up more. If you've traveled a lot, you've probably noticed this when some random Dutch person you meet for fifteen minutes on a bus ride offers to have you stay with his family if you're ever in Rotterdam. There's something about travel that helps you take down some of your normal defenses and open up. And when you open up, you connect with people on another level. There's also something about having a common goal (like hiking to the top of Half Dome) and being out of your familiar world that causes people to open up and be honest about their lives. When we share struggles together, life change starts to happen. I'm convinced this change is a direct result of a willingness to be vulnerable.

Love slows down to be vulnerable.

Naked and Unafraid

Dr. Brené Brown has studied vulnerability for years. In one study, she asked participants to describe what vulnerability feels like. She wrote, "The answer that appeared over and over in all our efforts to better understand vulnerability? Naked."[1]

We've all had those horrible dreams where we're running naked and couldn't find our clothes. That's what emotional vulnerability feels like. One of the things I learned early on in counseling was to not allow people to get too vulnerable in our first meeting. I'd ask them lots of questions, they'd respond, unload emotionally, get tons of insight, maybe cry a little, then never check back with me. I had one person write and apologize for being too open in one meeting. I realized that too much vulnerability right at the start made them feel embarrassed. It felt totally liberating for them to pour out all the frustration and anxiety that had been building inside them, but they felt naked and vulnerable afterward. So they ran and hid.

If you've opened your heart to someone before and have been hurt, there's a good chance you've decided vulnerability is dangerous. You have good reason to be cautious. I understand. The problem is that if you refuse to let others in, you will become increasingly isolated and alone. Being vulnerable feels risky, but it can actually release you from resentment, shame, and anger. When you feel known—in all your flaws and weaknesses—but still feel loved, that's a safe, connected, and empowering feeling. That's a picture of how God loves us. That's real, unconditional love.

Adam and Eve hid when they realized they were vulnerable. And we've all been hiding ever since. We don't want people to see how insecure we feel. The sad thing is, the reality that we're all in the same boat should draw us together—but instead, it tends to push us apart. We believe the lie that we're alone and nobody feels the way we do.

Nothing opens the door to a relationship quicker than realizing that you have something in common with the other person. There's nothing as liberating as hearing someone share their struggles with raising difficult kids, being hurt, addictions, or guilt and being able to finally admit: "Me too!" You stop being so hard on yourself as you realize you aren't alone.

One of the big mantras of counseling is this: it's the relationship that heals. The simple act of being open about your struggles with another person has a healing effect. Which is really good news, because it means we don't need any special training to help people. If we'll really be present, listen, and be honest about our own struggles, we have the ability both to be healed and be the healer. Henri Nouwen called this being "wounded healers." Fear and anger can't survive in that kind of environment.

The Enemy of Vulnerability

Recently, I spent two hours in a gut-wrenching conversation with a tearful individual who shared that he had just lost his apartment because he couldn't pay the rent. His long-term romantic relationship had just ended a few days earlier in the worst possible way. And to top it all off, he had just been fired from his job the day before. This person was struggling in a major way. But just a few short hours after that conversation, that same person posted a picture of himself drinking a cocktail and reclining in the sun by a glimmering pool with the hashtags "#pooltime #lifeisgood". Seriously. I couldn't figure out whether to laugh or cry. Lots of people commented with "I'm jealous" or "I wish I had your life." The picture was framed in such a way that you couldn't tell it was taken at a fleabag motel that the person had moved into because he had nowhere else to live. It looked glamorous, but that person's life was in shambles.

I love social media. But it can be the enemy of vulnerability. Social media—all media, in fact—only gives a partial picture of reality. It's deceptive. We can edit a picture to cover over parts we don't want people to see. Sometimes the way the final product is edited or filtered presents a downright lie. Unfortunately, often we become unknowing participants in that lie, and it actually leads to isolation and loneliness—the exact opposite of what we all want.

Social media often becomes an outlet where we try to convince ourselves that things are better than they actually are. I don't believe the person who posted that poolside picture was trying to be deceptive. I believe that person was actually trying to convince himself that life was good in the middle of a horrible situation. There's value in focusing on the positive. The problem is that the picture was deceptive. It's sad to say, but I'm not surprised anymore when I hear a couple is getting a divorce right after they post tons of pictures from an epic vacation they just took. The vacation was their last-ditch effort to save the marriage. But it didn't work. Again, I don't think they were being intentionally deceptive. I really believe they were trying to convince themselves that things were going to be OK. But they unintentionally presented a false image. I hope I'm not getting too cynical, but I've pretty much concluded that the louder someone is on social media— even if all they share is good—the more they are struggling.

The worst part is, when we craft an image that leaves out the bad parts, it causes others to believe everything is good with us. Which creates isolation. It closes the door to what could truly bring us healing: vulnerability. Sure, some people try to get vulnerable on social media, but it rarely works out well. People tend to unfriend those people who are constantly sharing all their problems. "I don't have emotional space for all this negativity, man."

Bottom line: Social media is not the best space for vulnerability. Vulnerability is most powerful in the context of familiarity. And familiarity tends to take time. It takes investment. It takes personal interaction. It takes getting to know the other person's story.

The Power of Your Story

Several years ago, I started coaching a couple who wanted help launching a marriage ministry. Earlier in this book, I discussed how important it is to figure out the *why* of your anger and frustration. *Why* always comes before *what* or *how*. The same is true when you feel called to start something new. Always start with your *why*—that's your engine. Your *why* tends to come from your personal story. It's your driving force and will help you persist when things get hard.

I kept asking for a *why* from this couple, but I was only getting what they were going to do and how they were going to do it. After over an hour of asking questions and hearing about marriage retreats and conferences, I finally asked, "What are you not telling me?"

They looked at each other nervously. One whispered, "Is it too soon to tell him?"

"Tell me! For goodness' sake. You're paying money for this. Let's not waste your time or money."

They hesitated. "Well, we both cheated on each other earlier in our marriage. But the Lord restored our marriage."

That was it. That was their *why*. They were passionate about marriage ministry because they had seen the pain and hurt that came from infidelity. But they had also seen miraculous restoration.

"There it is," I said. "When you tell that story, it's going to bring a lot of people hope and encouragement."

They both looked horrified. The husband spoke up. "Oh, no, no, no. We don't want to revisit that experience. It was too painful."

I spent the next few months helping them realize that their willingness to be transparent about their struggles—specifically, trying to help those who had suffered through the pain of infidelity—is what would bring authenticity to their marriage ministry.

A person with experience is never at the mercy of a person with theory. They could spend an entire retreat repeating lots of truth and tips about how to make a strong marriage, but if this couple really wanted to connect with those who were struggling, they needed to be honest and vulnerable about the entire story of God's work in their lives. The same is true for all of us.

There's a verse in Revelations that talks about God's children winning victory over their enemy through "the Blood of the Lamb and the word of their testimony."[2] Jesus's death and resurrection give us freedom and forgiveness. But it doesn't stop there. It has ongoing power. The power to help others win their own victory comes when we're willing to tell our story, our testimony—the good, bad, and ugly. When you're transparent and vulnerable about your struggles, it helps you see you aren't alone. It also helps others see they aren't alone. When you can admit your faults, it helps others come out from hiding.

James talked about the strength that comes from this kind of confession when he wrote, "Confess your sins to one another and pray for one another, that you may be healed."[3] When we confess to God for missing the mark, He forgives us. But sometimes we don't feel forgiven. That's why sharing our struggles with others is so important. I like how Rick Warren describes the power of confession: "If you want to be forgiven, you tell God. If you want to feel forgiven, you've got to tell one other person."[4] When you are willing to be honest about your struggles and victory, it gives hope to others.

Back to the Garden

When Adam and Eve were separated from God—the true source of security, connection, and empowerment—it made them afraid. They realized they were vulnerable. We all feel that deep fear of being vulnerable. It's normal. But living in that state just leads to anger and anxiety. The amazing thing is that because of Jesus's gift of love on the cross, we don't have to be afraid of being vulnerable anymore.

We are loved. Jesus committed the greatest act of love by giving His life for ours. When we walk with others in honesty and openness, we're actually expressing our confidence in God's love. We know we aren't what we should be, but because of Jesus's love, we aren't what we used to be. And the best is yet to come. In many ways, vulnerability is actually a way to let God's love flow through you into those around you. You don't need to hide. You can be honest. When you're honest, it helps others feel safe about being honest. It leads us on a path toward confidence and freedom. You don't have to hide from your past. God is redeeming it. So be honest about it and rejoice in His work in your life. Let others see the hope that comes through redemption. Your life is a story of God's redemption. Put your story out there on display for others to see. God will get glory, and you'll get joy.

And that leads us to the ultimate result of everything we've talked about so far.

Gratitude.

Be Grateful

*I would maintain that thanks are the highest
form of thought;
and that gratitude is happiness doubled by wonder.*

—G.K. Chesterton

The Kalalau Trail runs along the breathtaking Na Pali Coast on the Hawaiian island of Kauai. All along the trail there's dense jungle, some amazing waterfalls, and crystal-clear streams running into the ocean. When I took a team hiking there a few years back, there were even whales breaching and splashing in the deep blue waters of the Pacific. It was paradise.

I had been looking forward to this hike for years. We started early and covered a lot of ground in the first few hours, but just a few miles in, it started raining. It made the trail really muddy and difficult to hike. As the day went on, I started to realize that we were moving way too slowly to complete the distance I had planned that first day. This meant the entire plan for the hike would be thrown off. I was really frustrated and disappointed.

That evening at camp, while I was lying in my tent all annoyed and grumpy, listening to the raindrops falling, I had a realization: *You're in Hawaii! Pull yourself together, man!* This was a dream vacation for millions of people. And honestly, I was the only one on the team who seemed upset. Everyone else was just enjoying being in paradise. After all, we were camping in a Hawaiian jungle right next to a beautiful stream fed by a waterfall. Sure it was raining, but other than that, we had amazing weather. To top it off, it was January. Half the United States was being pummeled by snow. But in Hawaii, it was seventy degrees outside. I shifted my perspective and started enjoying the wonder of where I was and what I was doing.

I'm the world's best at focusing on one negative thing and letting it ruin all the good around me. No matter how great life is, I can zero in on the one thing that isn't just right. The worst part is that I let that one little thing cloud my ability to see all the good around me.

We're all prone to doing the same. You have a great job, but lately, one particular co-worker has made going to work feel miserable. You have a healthy, energetic child, but keeping an eye on that child is exhausting. You have a great car, but your neighbor just got a new one that's all shiny and doesn't have any scratches or dents. You start to feel discontented with the car you have.

No matter how great life gets, there's always something that isn't as perfect as it could be. Focusing on that one imperfect thing has a way of ruining even the best moments. It leads to all sorts of discontentment and negativity. But there is one decision that can clear the clouds and rain in our minds and help us see things as they really are. That decision is choosing gratitude.

Gratitude stops frustration, anger, and anxiety dead in their tracks. In fact, gratitude is the foundation for mental health. Gratitude is a decision to shift your perspective and focus on what's right in your life, rather than what's wrong.

Love slows down to be grateful.

Selective Abstraction

A while back, I spoke at a chapel for a Christian college. The auditorium was packed with students. I felt pretty young, so I figured

I'd really connect with the audience. But about four minutes into my talk, a student in the second row pulled out headphones, put them in his ears, then closed his eyes and leaned back. A minute later, another student about three rows behind him pulled out a textbook and started studying. At this point, I was getting pretty frazzled. I had a hard time focusing on what I was saying because I kept watching those two goobers in the front.

When I was done, the chaplain dismissed the students. He came up to me with a big smile on his face. "Man, I've never seen them so engaged. Great job!"

Pfft! I didn't believe him. I spent the rest of the day convinced that I was a failure at public speaking. There were about a thousand students that paid attention to my talk, but I just couldn't stop thinking about those two people who made it clear they had no interest in what I was saying.

In psychology, we talk about something called selective abstraction. It's focusing on one negative thing to the exclusion of everything else. Ninety-nine percent of a particular event may have been outstanding, but we're laser-focused on the one thing that went bad—like those two knuckleheads in my college talk.

There will always be something that isn't perfect in life. But gratitude holds its greatest power when we can be thankful, even when things aren't perfect. I say it's powerful because gratitude takes your eyes off of what's wrong and helps you focus on what's right.

And there's a lot that's right. In fact, for most of us reading this, it's really quite miraculous how good we have it. Most of us are way better off than our grandparents could have dreamed. In fact, most of us are better off than kings and queens from the past. We have indoor plumbing. We have electricity. We're living in a pretty great time.

It's so easy to take things for granted in life. In fact, often the things that were once seen as a blessing have become so normal that we just see them as a baseline for what we think we deserve. When we first got that dream job, it was a miracle; we called and told everyone about it. But eventually, that job became the new normal, and we started to forget what a gift it was. The same thing happens in marriages and relationships. Our spouses become a source of anger and frustration when we forget what a blessing it is to have someone who is committed to us.

Every blessing in your life comes with some burden. Blessings come with responsibility. Oftentimes the greatest responsibility is to just remind ourselves that what we have really is a blessing. Stay grateful for what seems normal. Because it's not. You are surrounded by miracles and amazing gifts, but you can miss them if you aren't thankful for them.

Getting through It with Gratitude

Recently, my daughter was sick for several days and required a lot of attention. She couldn't sleep for more than an hour, so neither could we. It was exhausting. We had to cancel some plans, and I couldn't get any work done. I remember feeling so frustrated and, at times, angry. *Will this ever end?!*

I decided I needed an attitude shift. I reminded myself: *It won't always be this way.* My daughter would get better. She was going to be back on her feet soon enough. I decided to focus on any good I could find in the situation. And I found it quickly. She was curled up next to me on the couch. She didn't squirm away or run off and play. She wanted to be near me. Sadly, I realized, it won't always be this way either. She won't be this small for long. She'll grow up and find her independence and won't need me anymore. It reminded me to be present and enjoy this while I can, even though her sickness wore me out. There's a burden and a blessing for every season. Shoulder the burden. Embrace the blessing. It won't always be this way.

Gratitude isn't ignoring the bad or acting like it doesn't exist. Gratitude is choosing to find what's good in the situation and focus on that. And there's always something good you can focus on. It might take a little work, but there is always something wonderful right around you that you may just have been taking for granted.

It goes back to focusing on "whatever is true, whatever is noble, whatever is right, whatever is pure, whatever is lovely, whatever is admirable—if anything is excellent or praiseworthy—think about such things."[1]

We talked about reframing your situation a few chapters ago. Gratitude is the ultimate tool for helping you reframe any situation. There are going to be some challenges in life that you just can't change. There are going to be some people you can't change and can't avoid. You just have to face them. But if you can find things to be grateful for in each situation, you can put a new frame around it.

Five months ago, I injured my hip while training for a hike, and it's still limiting what exercise I can do. I get frustrated about it a lot. While writing this chapter, I decided I needed to practice what I teach, so I started looking at what I could find to be grateful about from the injury. I have been trying to increase my flexibility for years. In order to keep my hip from tightening up, I have to do regular stretches. It's actually increasing my flexibility, and I've also found that it is improving my posture. I hate this injury, but I've started to see it in a new light, and I'm not quite as frustrated anymore.

What or who is the biggest cause for constant frustration or anger in your life right now? Think about it for a minute. What can you find that is positive in it? What's good about that person? What's the smallest thing for which you can be grateful? You don't have to drum up tons of gratitude. If you'll start small, it will grow from there. Once you nail it down, start being grateful for that one small thing. If you think your situation is just too horrible, and you can't find anything to be grateful for, here's my advice: aim lower. Keep searching for something to be grateful for, no matter how small, and your gratitude will grow from that small seed of gratitude.

Start Here

We've talked about a lot in this book—anger, fear, values, slowing down, priorities, letting go, and seeking solitude. Most of what we talked about just requires a new perspective. But if you've made it this far in the book and feel overwhelmed about where to start, then here's my simple tip.

Be grateful.

Start with gratitude. As medieval German theologian Meister Eckhart once said, "If the only prayer you said in your whole life was, 'Thank you,' that would suffice."

Slow down and make lots of space to be thankful for anything you can find.

Start naming what you're grateful for and why. If you really want it to sink in, say it out loud. You might even want to yell it. Spend the last few minutes before you go to bed writing down what went right that day. Say a prayer of thanks for all the good that happened and ask to be reminded of all the good around you. Start a journal where you keep track of all the good things God has done in your life.

Don't just keep the gratitude to yourself. Start expressing it. We tend to thank the waiter for refilling our glass more than we thank our spouses or co-workers for the little things they do. Change that. Be over the top with your gratitude. "But that's their job," you say. Sure, it may be. But thank goodness they're doing their jobs! We all know people who aren't doing their jobs; at least these people are! And besides all that, you know you love it when someone acknowledges that you are doing your job well. So express the gratitude to others that you wish they would give to you. It will start a chain reaction of gratitude. It will make everyone a little happier and a lot less angry and frustrated.

Start with gratitude and you'll be amazed at what starts to change in your life.

And that, my friends, is where we end this journey. Or maybe I should say, this is where we really start the journey. Living a real, full life of loving God and others starts with slowing down, consulting your anger, facing your fear, letting it go, embracing solitude, and walking with others. You don't have to be angry. You don't have to live with fear and anxiety. You don't have to be constantly running and trying harder. There's a big world full of love and joy and peace out there for you.

Slow down and enjoy it.

Acknowledgments

I'm so grateful for all the people who made this book possible.

Emily, I'm constantly reminded of what a perfect gift from God you are to me. I'm grateful for your love, joy, and strength.

Rick and Jana Malm, the older I get, the more I realize how fortunate I am to have parents like you. Thank you for your faithfulness in raising your kids with a passion for seeking God's kingdom first.

Drs. David and Vicki Allen, your insight, wise words (including the title for this book), and open-handedness with your work have been blessings that I can never repay.

Marcus and Natalie, without your generosity and support, I don't think we could do what we are doing today. Thank you for believing in the call of God on Emily and me.

Blythe, thank you for helping me clarify this project and walking through its completion with me. You are the best.

Catherine Russell, my personal counselor, thank you for talking through the challenging times with me. So much of what I've learned about forgiveness came from your insights.

To all the Salem crew—Tim, Karla, Jennifer, and countless others—thanks for supporting and believing in this project!

Notes

Chapter 2
1. This list is adapted from David F. Allen, *Contemplation: Intimacy in a Distant World* (McLean, Virginia: Curtain Call Productions, LLC, 2004), 54.

Chapter 3
1. James 1:9.

Chapter 4
1. Psalm 4:4.
2. Ajai Raj, "Feeling Hot Can Fuel Rage," *Scientific American*, January 1, 2014, https://www.scientificamerican.com/article/feeling-hot-can-fuel-rage.

Chapter 5
1. 2 Timothy 1:7.

Chapter 6
1. Luke 7:18–23.
2. I'd encourage you to read *Disappointment with God* by Philip Yancey (Grand Rapids, Michigan: Zondervan, 1988) for a deeper discussion on disappointment in the life of Job. It's an amazing book that changed my views on God.

Chapter 7
1. Hebrews 13:5.
2. 2 Corinthians 5:17.
3. Romans 8:28.
4. Genesis 50:20.
5. Viktor E. Frankl, *Man's Search for Meaning: An Introduction to Logotherapy* (New York: Simon & Schuster, 1984).

Chapter 8
1. 1 Samuel 18:8.
2. 2 Timothy 1:7.

Chapter 9
1. Proverbs 29:18.
2. Luke 12:34.

3.   Genesis 4:6.

Chapter 10
1.   Ecclesiastes 3.
2.   Matthew 6:33.
3.   Matthew 22:36–40.
4.   John 3:16.
5.   Hebrews 11:4.

Chapter 11
1.   Teresa Amabile, Constance Noonan Hadley, and Steven J. Kramer,
     "Creativity under the Gun," *Harvard Business Review* (August 2002),
     https://hbr.org/2002/08/creativity-under-the-gun.
2.   Jacquelyn Smith, "72% of People Get Their Best Ideas in the Shower—Here's
     Why," Business Insider, January 14, 2016, https://www.businessinsider.com/
     why-people-get-their-best-ideas-in-the-shower-2016-1.

Chapter 12
1.   Charles Duhigg, *The Power of Habit: Why We Do What We Do in Life and
     Business* (New York: Random House, 2012).

Chapter 13
1.   Proverbs 19:11 (NIV).
2.   Proverbs 4:23 (NIV).

Chapter 14
1.   Tom Valeo, "Forgive and Forget," WebMD, n.d., https://www.webmd.com/
     mental-health/features/forgive-forget#1.
2.   Ibid.
3.   Matthew 18:33 (NIV).
4.   Luke 23:34 (NIV).

Chapter 15
1.   Hebrews 5:8.
2.   A. W. Tozer, *The Root of the Righteous* (Camp Hills, PA: Wingspread
     Publishers, 2007.

Chapter 16
1.   Donna R. Addis, Christina M. Leclerc, Keely A. Muscatell, and Elizabeth A.
     Kensinger, "There Are Age-Related Changes in Neural Connectivity during
     the Encoding of Positive, but Not Negative, Information," *Cortex* 46, no. 4

(April 2010): 425–33, https://www.sciencedirect.com/science/article/abs/pii/
S001094520900152X?via%3Dihub.

2. Ecclesiastes 7:10 (NIV).
3. Philippians 3:13.
4. Matthew 9:17.

Chapter 17

1. Thomas Merton, *Thoughts in Solitude* (New York: Farrar, Straus, and
   Giroux, 1956, 1958).
2. Psalm 46:10.
3. Broadband Search, "Average Time Spent Daily on Social Media (Latest Data
   2020)," n.d., https://www.broadbandsearch.net/blog/
   average-daily-time-on-social-media.
4. Cal Newport, *Digital Minimalism: Choosing a Focused Life in a Noisy
   World* (New York: Portfolio, and imprint of Penguin Random House, 2019).
5. Daniel A. Gross, "This Is Your Brain on Silence," *Nautilus*, August 21, 2014,
   http://nautil.us/issue/16/nothingness/this-is-your-brain-on-silence.
6. Mark 4:26–27 (NLT).

Chapter 18

1. Genesis 2:7.
2. Chris Weller, "Japan Is Facing a 'Death by Overwork' Problem—Here's
   What It's All About," Business Insider, October 18, 2017, https://www.
   businessinsider.com/
   what-is-karoshi-japanese-word-for-death-by-overwork-2017-10.
3. Richard Foster, *The Celebration of Discipline* (London: Hodder and
   Stoughton, 1989).

Chapter 19

1. C.S. Lewis, *The Great Divorce* (New York: Macmillan Company, 1946).
2. James Fields, *Profiting from the Path of Most Resistance* (Friendswood,
   Texas: Wisdom House Publishers, 2003).
3. *TIME*'s Department, "The Hidden Secrets of the Creative Mind." *TIME*,
   January 16, 2006, http://content.time.com/time/magazine/
   article/0,9171,1147152,00.html.
4. Jonah Lehrer, *Imagine: How Creativity Works* (Edinburgh: Canongate
   Books, 2012).
5. Henri Nouwen, *Clowning in Rome* (New York: Doubleday, 1979).
6. Pierre Teilhard de Chardin, "Prayer of Teilhard de Chardin," in Michael
   Harter, ed., *Hearts on Fire: Praying with Jesuits* (Chicago: Loyola Press,
   2005).

Chapter 20
1.   1 Peter 5:8 (NIV).
2.   Psalm 1:2.
3.   James 1:5.
4.   Frederick Buechner, *Now and Then: A Memoir of Vocation* (New York: HarperCollins Publishers, 1983).
5.   Philippians 4:8.

Chapter 21
1.   Matthew 5:5.
2.   Shawn Achor, *The Happiness Advantage* (New York: Crown Publishing Group, 2010).

Chapter 22
1.   Matthew Killingsworth and Daniel Gilbert, "A Wandering Mind Is an Unhappy Mind," *Science*, November 11, 2010, http://www.danielgilbert.com/KILLINGSWORTH%20&%20GILBERT%20(2010).pdf.
2.   Stuart Wolpert, "Even When We're Resting, Our Brains Are Preparing Us to Be Social, UCLA Psychologists Report," UCLA Newsroom, May 28, 2015, http://newsroom.ucla.edu/releases/even-when-were-resting-our-brains-are-preparing-us-to-be-social-ucla-psychologists-report.
3.   J. M. Darley and C. D. Batson, "From Jerusalem to Jericho: A Study of Situational and Dispositional Variables in Helping Behavior," *JPSP* 27 (1973): 100–108, http://faculty.babson.edu/krollag/org_site/soc_psych/darley_samarit.html.

Chapter 23
1.   Brené Brown, *Daring Greatly* (New York: Avery, an imprint of Penguin Random House, 2012).
2.   Revelation 12:11.
3.   James 5:16.
4.   Rick Warren, "When We Confess, We Begin to Heal," PastorRick.com, March 5, 2017, https://pastorrick.com/when-we-confess-we-begin-to-heal/.

Chapter 24
1.   Philippians 4:8.